The Hierarchy of Saints

Part 1

The Hierarchy of Saints

Part 1

Spiritual Discourses of
Shaykh Muhammad Hisham Kabbani

PUBLISHED BY
INSTITUTE FOR SPIRITUAL AND CULTURAL ADVANCEMENT

Published and Distributed by:

Institute for Spiritual and Cultural Advancement (ISCA)
17195 Silver Parkway, #201
Fenton, MI 48430 USA
Tel: (888) 278-6624
Fax: (810) 815-0518
Email: staff@naqshbandi.org
Web: http://www.naqshbandi.org

First Edition: February 2013
THE HIERARCHY OF SAINTS, PART 1
ISBN: 978-1-930409-98-9

Library of Congress Cataloging-in-Publication Data

Kabbani, Muhammad Hisham.
Spiritual discourses of Shaykh Muḥammad Hisham Kabbani. -- 1st ed.
p. cm. -- "'The hierarchy of saints, part 1."
Includes bibliographical references.
ISBN 978-1-930409-98-9 (alk. paper)
1. Naqshabandiyah. 2. Sufism. I. Title.
BP189.7.N352K327 2013
297.4'8--dc22
2010044186

PRINTED IN THE UNITED STATES OF AMERICA
15 14 13 12 11 05 06 07 08 09

Mawlana Shaykh Hisham Kabbani inaugurates *Ramadan Series 2010* in the renowned Naqshbandi *zawiya* in Michigan where, since 1999, he continues the Ramadan tradition of reciting the *awrad* in congregation before sunrise, accompanied by an inspired spiritual discourse. The popular Ramadan program has been broadcast live on Sufilive.com since 2005 and reaches ten of thousands of viewers worldwide. (August 2010)

Table of Contents

About the Author

World-renowned religious scholar, Shaykh Muhammad Hisham Kabbani is featured in the ground-breaking book published by Georgetown University, *The 500 Most Influential Muslims in the World*. For decades he has promoted traditional Islamic principles of peace, tolerance, love, compassion and brotherhood, while rigorously opposing extremism in all its forms. He hails from a respected family of traditional Islamic scholars, which includes the former head of the Association of Muslim Scholars of Lebanon and the present grand mufti (highest Islamic religious authority) of Lebanon.

Shaykh Kabbani is highly trained, both as a western scientist and an Islamic scholar. He received a bachelor's degree in chemistry and later studied medicine. Under the instruction of Shaykh ʿAbdAllāh al-Fa'iz ad-Daghestani, upon whose personal notes this book is based, he holds a degree in Islamic Divine Law. Shaykh Muḥammad Nazim Adil al-Haqqani, world leader of the Naqshbandi-Haqqani Sufi Order, authorized him to guide students around the world in the ancient spiritual practices of Sufism.

In his long-standing endeavor to promote a better understanding of traditional Islam, in February 2010, Shaykh Kabbani hosted HRH Charles, the Prince of Wales at a cultural event at the revered Old Trafford Stadium in Manchester, U.K. He has hosted two international conferences in the U.S., and regional conferences on a host of issues, which attracted moderate Muslim scholars from Asia, the Far East, Middle East, Africa, U.K. and Eastern Europe. His counsel is sought by journalists, academics, policymakers and government leaders.

For thirty years, Shaykh Kabbani has consistently promoted peaceful cooperation among people of all beliefs. Since the early 1990s, he has launched numerous endeavors to bring moderate Muslims into the mainstream. Often at great personal risk, he has been instrumental in awakening Muslim social consciousness regarding the religious duty to stand firm against extremism and terrorism, for the benefit of all. Towards this goal, his bright, hopeful outlook and tireless campaign to spread the light of divine consciousness has helped millions understand the difference between moderate mainstream Muslims and minority extremist sects.

In the United States, Shaykh Kabbani serves as Chairman, Islamic Supreme Council of America; Founder, Naqshbandi Sufi Order of America;

Advisor, World Organization for Resource Development and Education; Chairman, As-Sunnah Foundation of America; and Founder, *The Muslim Magazine*. In the United Kingdom, Shaykh Kabbani is an advisor to Sufi Muslim Council, which consults to the British government on public policy and social and religious issues.

Other titles by Shaykh Kabbani include: *At the Feet of My Master* (2010, 2 vols.), *The Nine-fold Ascent* (2009), *Banquet for the Soul* (2008), *Illuminations* (2007), *Universe Rising* (2007), *Symphony of Remembrance* (2007), *A Spiritual Commentary on the Chapter of Sincerity* (2006), *The Sufi Science of Self-Realization* (Fons Vitae, 2005), *Keys to the Divine Kingdom* (2005), *Classical Islam and the Naqshbandi Sufi Order* (2004), *The Naqshbandi Sufi Tradition Guidebook* (2004), *The Approach of Armageddon? An Islamic Perspective* (2003), *Encyclopedia of Muḥammad's Women Companions and the Traditions They Related* (1998, with Dr. Laleh Bakhtiar), *Encyclopedia of Islamic Doctrine* (7 vols. 1998), *Angels Unveiled* (1996), *The Naqshbandi Sufi Way* (1995), *and Remembrance of God Liturgy of the Sufi Naqshbandi Masters* (1994).

Preface

This book is based on the divinely inspired spiritual discourses of the global head of the Naqshbandi-Haqqani Sufi Order, Mawlana Shaykh Nazim Adil al-Haqqani, and his representative, Mawlana Shaykh Hisham Kabbani. It is a compilation of Shaykh Kabbani's *suḥbah* from the annual "Ramadan Series" of 2010, which is devoted to ancient sacred teachings of the eminent Sufi masters of the famed Naqshbandi Golden Chain.

The Hierarchy of Saints, Part 1 contains in-depth descriptions of the hierarchy, responsibilities, powers, and character of *awlīyāullāh,* God's saints, and how they purify hearts of their followers and take them to the Divine Presence, which is the core of Sufi teachings.

Lessons of previous masters and their students offer the seeker a road map to success.

In this volume, learn the value and power of submitting wholeheartedly to the master; how to abandon your expectations and subjugate the ego to make quick progress in your spiritual journey; how to identify the false masters and avoid their traps; become familiar with tricks of your own ego that will lead you to stray from the Sufi path.

This title is recommended for anyone engaged in the study Sufism.

Publisher's Notes

This book is directed to those familiar with the Sufi Way; however, to accommodate lay readers unfamiliar with Sufi terminology and practices, we have provided English translations of Arabic texts and a comprehensive glossary. Where Arabic terms are crucial to the discussion, we have included transliteration and explanations. For readers familiar with Arabic and Islamic teachings, for further clarity please consult the cited sources.

The original material is based on transcripts of a series of holy gatherings known as *ṣuḥbah,* a divinely inspired talk given by the "shaykh," a highly trained spiritual guide. To present the authentic flavor of such rare teachings, great care was taken to preserve the speaking styles of both the author and the illustrious shaykhs upon whose notes this book is based.

Translations from Arabic to English pose unique challenges that we have tried our best to make understandable to Western readers. Please note our application of the common Arabic oral tradition of omitting definite articles such as "the Prophet" and "the Holy Qur'an," as practiced by Muslims around the world as intimate references.

We apply contemporary American English publishing standards and therefore do not italicize commonly known foreign nouns (jihād, Qur'an, shaykh) unless they appear in transliterations.

Quotes from the Holy Qur'an and Holy Traditions of Prophet Muḥammad are offset, italicized and cited.

The pronoun "they" is frequently used by Sufi guides to reference heavenly beings and holy souls who support them and give them orders, a usage that appears throughout this book. Where gender-specific pronouns such as "he" and "him" are applied in a general sense, no discrimination is intended towards women, upon whom The Almighty bestowed great honor.

Islamic teachings are primarily based on four sources, in this order:

- **Holy Qur'an**: the Islamic holy book of divine revelation (God's Word) granted to Prophet Muḥammad. Reference to Holy Qur'an appears as "4:12," which indicates "Chapter 4, Verse 12."
- **Sunnah**: holy traditions of Prophet Muḥammad ﷺ; the systematic recording of his words and actions that comprise the *ḥadīth.* For

fifteen centuries, Islam has applied a strict, highly technical standard, rating each narration in terms of its authenticity and categorizing its "transmission." As this book is not highly technical, we simplified the reporting of *ḥadīth,* but included the narrator and source texts to support the discussion at hand.

- ***Ijma*ʿ:** the adherence, or agreement of the experts of independent reasoning *(āhl al-ijtihād)* to the conclusions of a given ruling pertaining to what is permitted and what is forbidden after the passing of the Prophet, Peace be upon him, as well as the agreement of the Community of Muslims concerning what is obligatorily known of the religion with its decisive proofs. Perhaps a clearer statement of this principle is, "We do not separate (in belief and practice) from the largest group of the Muslims."
- **Legal Rulings:** highly trained Islamic scholars form legal rulings from their interpretation of the Qur'an and the Sunnah, known as *ijtihād.* Such rulings are intended to provide Muslims an Islamic context regarding contemporary social norms. In theological terms, scholars who form legal opinions have completed many years of rigorous training and possess degrees similar to a doctorate in divinity in Islamic knowledge, or in legal terms, hold the status of a high court or supreme court judge, or higher.

The following universally recognized symbols have been respectfully included in this work. While they may seem tedious, they are deeply appreciated by a vast majority of our readers.

ﷻ *Subḥānahu wa Taʿalā* (may His Glory be Exalted), recited after the name "Allāh" and any of the Islamic Names of God.

ﷺ *SallAllāhu ʿalayhi wa sallam* (God's blessings and greetings of peace be upon him), recited after the holy name of Prophet Muḥammad.

ؑ *ʿAlayhi ʿs-salām* (peace be upon him/her), recited after holy names of other prophets, names of Prophet Muḥammad's relatives, the pure and virtuous women in Islam, and angels.

ؓ/ؓ *RaḍīAllāhu ʿanh(um)* (may God be pleased with him/her), recited after the holy names of Companions of Prophet Muḥammad; plural: *raḍīAllāhu ʿanhum.*

ق represents *QaddasAllāhu sirrah* (may God sanctify his secret), recited after names of saints.

Transliteration

Transliteration from Arabic to English poses challenges. To show respect, Muslims often capitalize nouns that appear in English in lowercase.

To facilitate authentic pronunciation of names, places and terms, use the following key:

Symbol	Transliteration	Symbol	Transliteration	Vowels: Long	
ء	'	ط	ṭ	آ ى	ā
ب	b	ظ	ẓ	و	ū
ت	t	ع	ʿ	ي	ī
ث	th	غ	gh	Short	
ج	j	ف	f	َ	a
ح	ḥ	ق	q	ُ	u
خ	kh	ك	k	ِ	i
د	d	ل	l		
ذ	dh	م	m		
ر	r	ن	n		
ز	z	ه	h		
س	s	و	w		
ش	sh	ي	y		
ص	ṣ	ة	ah; at		
ض	ḍ	ال	al-/'l-		

Masters of the Naqshbandi-Haqqani Golden Chain

May Allāh ﷻ preserve their secrets.

1. Prophet Muḥammad ibn ʿAbdAllāh ﷺ
2. Abū Bakr as-Ṣiddīq ق
3. Salmān al-Farsi ق
4. Qasim bin Muḥammad bin Abū Bakr ق
5. Jafar aṣ-Ṣādiq ق
6. Tayfur Abū Yazīd al-Bistāmi ق
7. AbūlHassan ʿAlī al-Kharqani ق
8. Abū ʿAlī al-Farmadi ق
9. Abū Yaqub Yusuf al-Hamadani ق
10. AbūlAbbas, al-Khiḍr ق
11. ʿAbdul Khāliq al-Ghujdawāni ق
12. Arif ar-Riwakri ق
13. Khwaja Maḥmūd al-Anjir al-Faghnawi ق
14. ʿAlī ar-Ramitani ق
15. Muḥammad Baba as-Samasi ق
16. as-Sayyid Amir Kulal ق
17. Muḥammad Bahaʿuddin Shah Naqshband ق
18. Alaʿuddin al-Bukhāri al-Attar ق
19. Yaqub al-Charkhi ق
20. Ubaydullāh al-Ahrar ق
21. Muḥammad az-Zahid ق
22. Darwish Muḥammad ق
23. Muḥammad Khwaja al-Amkanaki ق
24. Muḥammad al-Baqi billāh ق
25. Aḥmad al-Farūqi as-Sirhindi ق
26. Muḥammad al-Masum ق
27. Muḥammad Sayfuddin al-Farūqi al-Mujaddidi ق
28. as-Sayyid Nūr Muḥammad al-Badawani ق
29. Shamsuddin Habib Allāh ق
30. ʿAbdAllāh ad-Dahlawi ق
31. Khālid al-Baghdādī ق
32. Ismail Muḥammad ash-Shirwāni ق
33. Khas Muḥammad Shirwāni ق
34. Muḥammad Effendi al-Yaraghi ق
35. Jamāluddin al-Ghumuqi al-Ḥusayni ق
36. Abū Aḥmad as-Sughuri ق
37. Abū Muḥammad al-Madani ق
38. Sharafuddīn ad-Daghestani ق
39. ʿAbdAllāh al-Faʿiz ad-Daghestani
40. Muḥammad Nazim Adil al-Haqqani ق

Recitation before Every Association

بسم الله الرحمن الرحيم

A'ūdhu billāhi min ash-Shayṭān ir-rajīm.
Bismillāhi' r-Raḥmāni 'r-Raḥīm.
Nawaytu 'l-arbā'īn, nawaytu 'l-'itikāf,
nawaytu'l-khalwah, nawaytu 'l-'uzlah,
nawaytu 'r-riyāḍa, nawaytu 's-sulūk,
lillāhi Ta'alā fī hādhā 'l-masjid.

Atī'ūllāha wa ati' ūr-Rasūla
wa ūli'l-amri minkum.

I seek refuge in Allāh from Satan, the rejected.
In the Name of Allāh, the Merciful,
the Compassionate.
I intend the forty (days of seclusion);
I intend seclusion in the mosque,
I intend seclusion, I intend isolation,
I intend discipline (of the ego); I intend to travel
in God's Path for the sake of God,
in this mosque.

Obey Allāh, obey the Prophet,
and obey those in authority among you.
Sūratu 'n-Nisa (The Women), 4:59

Purify My House

A'ūdhu billāhi min ash-Shayṭāni 'r-rajīm. Bismillāhi' r-Raḥmāni 'r-Raḥīm.
Nawaytu 'l-arba'īn, nawaytu 'l-'itikāf, nawaytu'l-khalwah, nawaytu 'l-'uzlah,
nawaytu 'r-riyāḍa, nawaytu 's-sulūk, lillāhi Ta'alā fī hādhā 'l-masjid.
Atī'ūllāha wa atī'ū 'r-Rasūla wa ūli 'l-amri minkum. (4:59)

This Ramadan, *inshā'Allāh* we will see a lot of changes and especially spiritual changes in the hearts of *murīds* of *awlīyāullāh*; more changes will be in the hearts of *murīds* of Sulṭān al-Awlīyā, Mawlana Shaykh Nazim al-Haqqani ق, who gave permission to speak on his behalf these kinds of lectures or this kind of knowledge in this Ramadan. Mawlana Shaykh Nazim mentioned to me to speak about the importance of *awlīyāullāh* in the life of human beings.

Allāh ﷻ said in the Holy Qur'an:

Wa ṭāhhir baytī lil 'akifīn wa-ruka' us-sujūd.
Sanctify My House for those who compass it round, or stand up, or bow, or prostrate themselves (therein in prayer). (Sūrat al-Ḥajj, 22:26)

It means Allāh is giving an order to Sayyīdina Ibrāhīm ⸙, all the way to Sayyīdina Muḥammad ﷺ, "Purify My House"; purify the status of the House, to make it ready for people to circumambulate it. Everything is pure, even the mass: the mass is what Allāh ﷻ created; this physical body is the mass and the house of the soul. The atom is the house, the mass of the electron, and since the mass is pure, the electrons circumambulate the mass; the electrons will not circumambulate if the mass is not pure or then everything will be still, with no life.

Allāh made everyone circumambulate a purified House of Allāh. The bees circumambulate their queen, birds circumambulate their mother and father, children circumambulate their parents. And Allāh ﷻ has made the soul in the body circumambulate a purified house in the body, and that is why Allāh said, *wa ṭāhhir baytī*, "Purify My House," to Sayyīdina Ibrāhīm ⸙, and Sayyīdina Isma'īl ⸙, and all prophets ⸙, for the *tāifīn*, those who circumambulate the House, and the *'akifīn*, those who withdrew from *dunyā* or something they like, and everyone likes *dunyā*. But the *'akifīn* that Allāh mentions in Holy Qur'an are those *awlīyāullāh* who are away, but they are *ʿakifin;* it means they sit and withdraw from *dunyā.*

The first level of *awlīyāullāh* is comprised of those who circumambulate in constant motion around the House. Those who are on a lesser level are withdrawing and doing *dhikrūllāh,* remembering Allāh through their hearts, but not circumambulating and standing. And the third level are those who are in *rukʿū* and prostrating in *sujūd.* "Clean My House," is meant for those who are in these three categories: who circumambulate continuously, who are not in *dunyā,* sitting, and those who are in *rukʿū* and *sujūd.*

That message applies to the House of Allāh ﷻ. Allāh made His angels make *sajda* to whom? To make *sajda* for the light of Sayyīdinā Muḥammad ﷺ that appeared in the forehead of Sayyīdinā Adam ؑ. That is why Imām Malik ؓ said to the *amīr* of that time, "Don't turn your face to the *qiblah* in Madinah, turn it to the Prophet ﷺ, the one who took you to Allāh's House." So turning your face to Prophet ﷺ is the place where *awlīyāullāh* are circumambulating.

The *Ṣaḥābah* ؓ circumambulated the Prophet ﷺ, as his heart is the House of Allāh. The revelation of the message did not come on the *Kaʿbah,* it came on the heart of the Prophet, so that heart is what Prophet has given pure for the *ummah* to circumambulate.

Awlīyāullāh are inheritors from the Prophet ﷺ, so they have a direction for their *murīds* to run to them, to circumambulate their hearts, as it is the House of Allāh.

Prophet ﷺ said in *Ḥadīth Qudsī*[1]:

Qalb al-mu'min baytu 'r-rabb.
The heart of the believer is the House of the Lord.

Mā wasiʿanī arḍī wa lā samā ' ī lākin wasiʿanī qalbi ʿabdī al-mu'min.
Neither Earth nor Heavens contained Me, but the heart of the believer contained Me.

So your direction is to find one of these purified hearts that you can withdraw from *dunyā* and do *murāqabah,* meditation, to them and they will take you to the presence of Prophet ﷺ, and you must always keep their

[1] What Allāh ﷻ spoke directly to Prophet Muhammad ﷺ.

respect. An example of that is when someone asked one of the *awlīyāullāh*, "Can you tell me about the level of Sayyīdinā Abdul Qadir al-Jilani? What is his *maqām*?"

That *walī* said, "One time Sayyīdinā Abdul Qadir al-Jilani was asked, 'Who is your shaykh?'"

Man lā shaykha lahu shaykhahu 'sh-Shayṭān.
Who doesn't have a guide, his desires will be Shayṭān.

Because without a shaykh you cannot decide; you might see something wrong as correct and the correct as wrong. Sometimes the shaykh tells you, "Do this," and to you and to many others it is not correct, but to the shaykh it has *ḥikmah*, wisdom. You don't know the wisdom and they can see farther than you, and you will know the wisdom later, so don't object. What do we do? We complain and object; that order doesn't click in our mind. We think, "Why is he telling me to do this? It is *ḥarām*." Do you know better than the shaykh if it is *ḥarām* or *halāl*? No. So what must you do? Surrender!

Who Is Your Shaykh?

One time they asked Sayyīdinā Abdul Qadir al-Jilani ق, "Who is your shaykh?"

He said, "A long time ago I had a shaykh, Sayyid Hammad ad-Dībās, but today it changed." Because Sayyīdinā Abdul Qadir al-Jilani ق kept respect to his shaykh and he went very high, and after his shaykh left *dunyā* he became an inheritor and he reached higher levels. He said, "Today I am receiving knowledge from two oceans."

Look at how *awlīyāullāh* receive knowledge; not like us, because their hearts are purified. They buy machines today, saying, "This machine is a purifier." Purifier of what? Purifier of the pet dander that you cannot see, but it is there; it means the bad desires. You need a purifier to purify that animal dust and take it out, and then you need a humidifier to give you a nice breeze. So the heart of a *walī* purifies and humidifies the *murīd*, giving them that cool breeze at the end after purifying them.

The shaykh knows the hearts of his followers. He might look at you and see what you need to do and he wants to empty your heart, though it might not coincide with what you believe. So he asks you to do something specific as he wants to take that away.

Sayyīdinā Abdul Qadir al-Jilani ق said, "I receive from two oceans, *Baḥr an-Nubūwwah,* "the Ocean of the Heart of Prophet ﷺ," and from *Baḥr al-Futūwwah,* "the Ocean of Chivalry."

One is from the ocean of the Prophet ﷺ and one is from the ocean of Sayyīdinā ʿAlī ؓ, as Prophet ﷺ said:

Lā fatā illa ʿAlī wa lā sayf illa dhul-fiqār.
There is no chivalry except with Sayyīdinā ʿAlī and no sword except Dhul-fiqār (his sword from Heavens).

That means he was most powerful against his ego with his sword, not only on unbelievers. Mawlana Shaykh always tells us a story about Sayyīdinā ʿAlī ؓ, when he was in battle, one of the unbelievers, a very strong wrestler, called Sayyīdinā ʿAlī bad names. Then they fought in one-on-one combat and afterwards the armies fought directly, not like today when soldiers don't even see the enemy. There is no chivalry today; they blow them up from far away. That is not chivalry, it is cowardice. And so, Sayyīdinā ʿAlī put him down and in war when you put someone down you have the right to kill him. So that wrestler said, "Okay, kill me!" and then he spat in the face of Sayyīdinā ʿAli. Immediately Sayyīdinā ʿAlī threw the sword down.

Again he said, "Kill me!"

Sayyīdinā ʿAlī ؓ replied, "I cannot as I became angry and then it will not be for sake of Allāh."

Then that wrestler said, "If your religion is like that, then I will become Muslim." Then he took from the heart of Prophet ﷺ and the heart of Sayyīdinā ʿAlī ؓ!

So there was a question that remained, just as today it stays in the hearts of *murīds*. They ask, "What is your shaykh's level?" We answer, "It is Sulṭān al-Awlīyā and he takes from the heart of the Prophet ﷺ." So that questioned remains until now.

They asked Sayyīdinā Imām Abu 'l-Hasan al-Shādhilī ق, a very famous *walī* buried in Egypt, "Who is your shaykh?" and he said, "My shaykh was Sayyīdinā ʿAbd as-Salam ibn Mashīsh ق," a very famous shaykh from Morocco, a big *walī*. "I used to receive knowledge from his heart and circumambulate his heart and sit looking at him, and I withdrew from *dunyā* looking at him and making *rukʿū* and *sujūd* in his presence. But today I am receiving from ten different oceans."

You don't understand how *awlīyā* are speaking; it depends on the time they are in. Today more *raḥmāh* is coming as we are in time of *fitna*. More of that power is coming to the *Ghawth* and passing to the five *quṭbs*, and that makes us able to see with his light, as he is taking from Prophet ﷺ, who is ascending so high. By looking with the power in their eyes, they can turn bad into good! With their strong laser-like vision they can purify people from all their diseases and clean them only by looking, hearing, or touching.

Then they asked him, "Who is your shaykh today?"

"It was ʿAbd as-Salām ibn Mashīsh, but today I am taking from ten oceans: five from Heavens and five from Earth. I am receiving from their hearts directly."

He was taking from the heart of Abū Bakr aṣ-Ṣiddīq ق whatever Prophet ﷺ poured in his heart. And from Sayyīdinā ʿUmar al-Farūq ؓ, who fought *bātil*, of which there is too much today. And from Sayyīdinā ʿUthmān ؓ and from Sayyīdinā ʿAli, *karamAllāhu wajah wa ʿalayhi ʿs-salām*, taking from five.

About Sayyīdinā ʿAli, Prophet ﷺ said:

ʿAna madinatu ʿl-ʿilmi wa ʿAliyyun babuha.
I am the city of knowledge and ʿAlī is its door. (al-Ḥākim, Tirmidhī)

And he ﷺ said, "Whatever I received, I poured in the heart of Abū Bakr." And ʿUmar was the one distinguishing *ḥaqq* from *bātil*. And Sayyīdinā ʿUthmān had two lights, two daughters of Prophet ﷺ and he was so generous.

Allāh ﷻ said:

Taʿruju ʿl-malāʾikati wa ʿr-rūh u ilayhi fi yawim kāna miqdārahu khamsīn alfa sannah.
The Spirit and the angels ascend to Him in a day whose length is fifty thousand years. (Sūrat al-Maʿarij, 70:5)

He is receiving revelation from Jibrīl ؑ, and from Mikāʾīl ؑ who sends rain, from Isrāfīl ؑ who blows the trumpet (it means he receives the power of that), and from Azrāʾīl ؑ he receives power of the Afterlife, and from

"Rūh," the Angel of Souls, who carries all these souls. So this is how *awlīyā* receive their knowledge; they purified their hearts so their *murīds* can reach and take from that fountain in their hearts. And we have to know that to every *walī* Allāh ﷻ gave *khuṣūṣīyyah,* a specialization, a special job or way, unique to that *walī;* it is not the same to another *walī.*

Everyone has a different way, a different *mashrab,* fountain, and that fountain is like *naqsh ʿalā hajr,* engraving on stone, which is permanent and never disappears. So one *walī* knows another from what is engraved on his heart. That is why there are Ninety-nine Beautiful Names and Attributes, and from them the names of high-level *walīs* are engraved on his heart. So like *Allāhu lā ilāha illa Hūwa 'r-Raḥmānu 'r-Raḥīm,* Abdur-Raḥmān is receiving that knowledge from that secret of the Divine Name, "Ar-Raḥmān," and Abdur-Raḥīm is receiving from the Divine Name, "Ar-Raḥīm." We will explain them later, one by one.

As their hearts are purified, Allāh ﷻ is throwing in their hearts from *'Āḥadiyya,* "the Ocean of Unique Oneness," and *Wāḥidiyya,* "the Ocean of Oneness." And especially in *Ṭarīqah Naqshbandiyyah,* we are receiving from an ocean that takes you to *Maqām al-Fanā,* "the Station of Annihilation," which Sayyīdinā Shah Naqshband ق pulled from heart of Prophet ﷺ.

That is why the *ṭarīqah* takes from his name, as he was able to take from secrets of these engravings, that every *walī* has a name, and he exposed them from a level we can understand, and it is a different level for each *walī* depending on the level in which he receives knowledge. There are *awlīyā* that stand at the feet of prophets, which means they receive directly from hearts of prophets. There are 124,000 prophets and there is a *walī* receiving from each prophet, and there is one receiving from the heart of Prophet Muḥammad ﷺ.

This is an introduction to what we will be speaking about this Ramadan, and I hope we can continue as much as we can.

So during this discussion, they asked Sayyīdinā Abdul Qadir al-Jilani ق from where he received his knowledge, and they asked Sayyīdinā Abū 'l-Ḥasan al-Shādhilī ق, and then they asked Sayyīdinā Abū Madyan ash-Shādhilī ق, who said, "I have *juld,* I traveled in knowledges of Allāh's Kingdom, and that is 101 oceans of knowledges.

Grandshaykh ʿAbdAllāh ad-Daghestani ق said what we will explain tomorrow *inshā'Allāh,* "To *awlīyāullāh* in this time, on every letter of Holy Qur'an, Allāh ﷻ opened from 12,000 to 24,000 oceans of knowledge that He will open to your heart and guide you through spiritual navigation."

As you navigate today with GPS, Allāh will navigate you with heavenly navigation, but only your soul knows, not your body, as they cannot open those secrets to our bodies. So that is coming to the hearts of *murīds* like a drizzle, dripping from different sides like a shower, so you get heavenly knowledges they throw in your heart to navigate you. Your soul understands, as you have *baya*ʿ with the shaykh, so Mawlana Shaykh is navigating our souls, but not openly; some are getting like a drizzle, some like a shower, and some receive like a thunderstorm.

May Allāh ﷻ forgive us and may Allāh ﷻ bless us.

Wa min Allāhi 't-tawfīq, bi ḥurmati 'l-ḥabīb, bi ḥurmati 'l-Fātiḥah.
And with Allāh is success. For the sake of the Beloved, for his sake we recite the opening chapter of Holy Qur'an.

Characteristics of the Abdal

A'ūdhu billāhi min ash-Shayṭāni 'r-rajīm. Bismillāhi' r-Raḥmāni 'r-Raḥīm. Nawaytu 'l-arbā'īn, nawaytu 'l-'itikāf, nawaytu'l-khalwah, nawaytu 'l-'uzlah, nawaytu 'r-riyāḍa, nawaytu 's-sulūk, lillāhi Ta'alā fi hādhā 'l-masjid. Atī'ūllāha wa atī'ū 'r-Rasūla wa ūli 'l-amri minkum. (4:59)

Allāh ﷻ created His *awlīyāullāh* of different ranks. No *walī* crosses his limits; he knows where he stands and he is happy with what Allāh gave him. Why don't they cross their limits? There is wisdom there. Allāh puts in their hearts that they have reached the top level, the top point, and they feel they are at that highest level. Although they might be in a lower level, to them it looks like the highest level. That is why they keep content and happy, or else there would have been a kind of unaccepted complaint from that *walī*, that he wants to go to see the rank of the other one. So Allāh ﷻ hides them from each other and gives them the feeling that they have reached the highest station.

That is why you see there are 124,000 *walīs* and everyone thinks he is taking directly from Prophet ﷺ, but in reality they are taking from the one directly above them in rank, and they are all eventually receiving from the *Ghawth,* the *"al-Fard al-Jami',"* who brings everyone together. There cannot be two or three who bring everyone together, there can only be one. And then going down to the level that Allāh ﷻ showed the beauty of the world of Jamāl, the Beautiful; when it is opened, they see beauty in everything, not only on Earth but in the universe, and when they reach it they cannot look at anything else but that beauty.

People here say there is competition in the arts, who is the best artist. From their drawings you can see this artist is better than that one. When *awlīyāullāh* see the beauty of what Allāh ﷻ created, they can no longer see that anything is not beautiful, so they are attracted to that beauty that Allāh ﷻ put in Earth and in Heavens.

When you admire people, when you open your heart to love people because you see that beauty, you are welcoming them through your arms and you are extending what you can give them in their lives. That beauty you see in them is the seed Allāh put, that small *tajallī* appearing through them. That is why the *walī* will be a magnet to them and even one look from him to them will take away their difficulties. And that *walī* will transfer that beauty to their hearts and give them a spiritual injection, so on the Day of Judgment they will be under his control.

Not only did Allāh ﷻ give them that beauty to use in order to reach the maximum number of people, but He makes them travel throughout his universes and this Earth, from one place to another, to see more and more of those people who are lost or not lost, to bring them to *Hazīrat al-Jamāl,* the Garden of Beauty. If anyone enters that Garden of Beauty, they cannot come out of it.

That group of *awlīyāullāh* who are under the *Ghawth* are five *quṭbs* (poles) that Allāh ﷻ established in *dunyā* to attract as many people as possible through their travels. They have power to travel through spiritual dimensions and they have power to travel throughout Earth. They can move through heavenly and earthly power and according to *ḥikmah* (wisdom) of Allāh ﷻ, they follow these two ways.

Allāh ﷻ has made their hearts the place in which they can see His secret, *wa atlaʿtahum ʿalā shams asrārahum.* In every secret there is a sun shining and every secret has been given to one of them. You cannot get the same secret the other one has or else it is not a secret. Allāh ﷻ gave each one a certain secret he has to follow in order to reach *ʿirādatullāh* (Will of Allāh). He made their souls holy and he made their bodies heavenly. These *awlīyāullāh* have a pure heavenly, subtle body so that they are able to receive these secrets from the Heavens. And they have an earthly body through which they deliver the message that Allāh is sending to them through Prophet Muḥammad ﷺ.

Allāh ﷻ gave those five *quṭbs,* with the *Ghawth,* who is the sixth at the top of them, the ability to mine. When you are searching for diamonds, you mine. You might go underground three-hundred feet or three-thousand feet to find diamonds. Allāh ﷻ gave them that power of mining in the hearts of people, to take away what is bad and evil and to put inside what is good.

Don't underestimate the power of a *walī*; they are able to reach from anywhere to anyone, but they prefer to show mostly their physical appearance, to see more people in need for support, and they support them. Allāh ﷻ gave them *Quwwat al-Mujāhadah,* the Power of Struggling, by putting Shayṭān down and putting *ḥaqq* (truth) in the hearts of people. Their lives are a struggle. They do not just sit, like many people who are lazy and their concern is only for this life, with no concern for the other life. So Allāh ﷻ has put in the hearts of these five *quṭbs* the Power to Struggle, to fight against Shayṭān, to remove *bātil* (falsehood) and to put *ḥaqq* in the hearts of people, and they can do this with the power of their eyes.

Sayyīdinā Aḥmad al-Badawī ق covered his eyes because anyone looking into his eyes fainted. When he reached the highest level possible, a *quṭb* came to him and said, "*Yā* Aḥmad! You need your trust, the key to that door. I have it."

He said, "I don't need the key from you, I need the key from Allāh."

The *quṭb* said, "Okay, try to get it on your own!"

He asked for that key and that *quṭb* disappeared. Finally, Aḥmad al-Badawī ق was hearing a voice coming to his heart, saying, "*Yā* Aḥmad! If you want that key, My key is with that *quṭb*. Go find him." And he went for six months looking for that *quṭb* and he didn't find him. That *quṭb* didn't appear; he was near him but Aḥmad al-Badawī was not seeing him. That *quṭb* didn't give him his key; instead he took all Aḥmad al-Badawī's knowledge, because it was based on his ego.

Show me today anyone who is not basing his knowledge on his ego. *ʿUlamā* today are so proud of their knowledge that they want to put in front of their names the title "Doctor." They want this not just for medical doctors, but so they are all *ʿalāmah*, a *pir*, a professor, a doctor, and that is from the ego. So most of today's *ʿulamā* are building their knowledge on their egos. *Awlīyāullāh* are building their knowledge on the Oceans of Prophet ﷺ that Allāh ﷻ is giving to him.

That is why Imām Muḥammad al-Busayrī ؓ said that everyone is taking from the Ocean of Prophet ﷺ. This is where we put our back, that is where our *ʿitimād* is: our support comes from Prophet ﷺ, our backbone, he supports us.

So these *aqtād* are highest in their levels. We won't elaborate that now; we will go through something else *inshā'Allāh*, but they are the highest of *awlīyā*, and when one goes his seat has to be filled immediately; it cannot remain empty. These five are: *Quṭb, Quṭb al-Bilād, Quṭb al-Aqtāb, Quṭb al-Irshād, Quṭb al-Mutaṣarrif.* With the eyes of their hearts and their head, all their attention is continuously focused on the *Ghawth*. They take their daily assignments from him and he connects everyone to him, and he is taking orders from Prophet ﷺ.

And that is why, as there are five *quṭbs,* there are also five groups of *awlīyā* under them: *Budalā, Nujabā, Nuqabā, Awtād,* and *Akhyār*. They are looking at the *quṭb's* order, to execute it. Allāh ﷻ made them *Āhlu 'l-Fadl*, the

People of Favor, and Allāh favors His servants. Therefore, they have to reach and share those heavenly favors with everyone.

So there is the *Ghawth,* five *quṭbs,* and under the five *quṭbs* are five different groups. First of them is "*Budalā,*" whom Allāh ﷻ made *Āhlu 'l-Fadl* and He made them so generous. They have to give to everyone, and they don't ask (about the state of that person); whether someone is saying the truth or not, they give *fī sābīlillāh,* in Allāh's Way.

They are always on *istiqāmah,* the Right Path. If you see something from them that you don't understand, don't object or you will lose, because they might do something your mind may not accept. But they know there is wisdom in it and their goals are there, because they are always on *istiqāmah,* the Right Path, so they know.

You might not always be on the Right Path; you might be on the diversion or the exit. The highway is straight and there are many exits. If you exit, you are not on the highway anymore. You cannot see what *awlīyāullāh* are seeing. You are exiting, maybe on the first or the second or the third exit. *Awlīyāullāh* don't exit. They stay on the straight highway, the Straight Path, *Ṣirāṭ al-Mustaqīm.*

So when you exit, you are looking from far away and you might not see what the *walī* on the highway is seeing. Don't try to balance what the *walī* knows to your mind because Allāh made these *'abdāl* to save themselves from imaginations, *khayāl. Takhallasū min al-khayālāt,* "They freed themselves from imagination." We normal people are full of imagination, like in the desert you see a mirage and you think you see an oasis of water, but you run and then you don't see anything. This is *wahm,* imagination, *khayāl.* A *walī* will see there is nothing there. That is why you need a guide; you cannot be alone.

Their Physical and Hidden Assignments

Allāh ﷻ gave them four different assignments that are physical and four hidden ones that are spiritual. The first physical one the *'abdāl* have is to keep quiet; they don't talk. It is like what Sayyīdinā 'Alī ؓ said. "To save yourself (from sin), first is not to talk, *aṣ-ṣamt.*" When you talk you begin to show you know nothing. What is 'not to talk'? It is not only not to talk to people, but to make your heart not talk against people by throwing them with *sūw al-khāṭir,* bad thoughts. It means not only through your tongue, but *ṣamt* has to be through your tongue and your heart.

How much do we accuse people through our hearts and speak badly about them? Always these *Shaytanic* gossips come to our hearts or our minds, and we begin to say things that violate the rights of others. So Allāh ﷻ gave the *ʿabdāl* the physical power to keep quiet and that is why you don't know them. They might be in your physical presence but you don't know them, it might be they come in the appearance of a man you know or you don't know, and they keep quite.

And second, Allāh gave them power of *sahr,* to stay up all night, not to sleep. Can you stay up all night? It is not only physical sleep, but also their hearts do not sleep; their hearts remain continuously in divine service.

As related by Aḥmad in his *Musnad,* Prophet ﷺ said, "When you are in the jungle or desert and feel afraid, call on *ʿibādAllāh, ʿabdāl,* the Substitutes, *rijālAllāh,* and they will come and support you."

Everywhere is a jungle; to be around people or in gatherings is a jungle of people with different beliefs, thoughts, actions, behaviors and ideas, and it is a jungle of bad, low desires. Allāh ﷻ gave the *ʿabdāl* power to go everywhere, because everywhere is a jungle; today there is no place pure on this *dunyā.*

Balad al-Ḥarām in Mecca is pure, and in Madinah it is pure, and in Masjid al-Aqsa it is pure, and in Shām (Damascus) it is pure; Allāh ﷻ gave us these. But even in these pure places, today people are not behaving correctly. It is a jungle, so they need *awlīyāullāh, ʿabdāl,* to reach them. They are taking orders from *quṭbs* and they do that. "Go here, go there, appear in this place and appear in that place." Sometimes they use normal, physical means and sometimes they use spiritual means. They don't like to show *karāmah,* miracles, they want to show normality to everyone.

Allāh ﷻ gave them the power of *sahr ʿalā rāḥat an-nās*. If a baby is sick in the hospital, you stay with her all night. They look after everyone through their spiritual means in order to lift up that one who is losing his faith or losing his duties during the day. They reach him and they don't differentiate from one to another, as they have orders to reach everyone in need.

Always, if there is food they eat and if there is no food they don't care, they don't eat. *Al-jūʿ* is one of their characteristics, hunger. They want to feel with everyone, that there are poor people with no food, to sympathize with them, they do not eat. And this I saw in Grandshaykh ق and in Mawlana Shaykh Nazim ق; they don't eat, but we run to fill our stomachs and graze.

They always seclude themselves. They have this characteristic of being away from people. When they need to appear, they appear, but otherwise they seclude themselves.

So they carry these characteristics, especially *aṣ-ṣamt,* which is to keep quiet. Their speech is only *dhikrūllāh.* You see always Allāh's Name on their tongue, either *dhikr* of *"Allāh, Allāh,"* or *"lā ilāha illa-Llāh,"* or *ṣalawāt* on Prophet ﷺ.

They don't sleep because they are busy during the nights reaching people when everyone is sleeping. And also, the spiritual meaning of sleeping is *ghaflah,* to be heedless, and they don't allow themselves to be heedless. They are always looking at the five *quṭbs,* and the five *quṭbs* are always looking at the *Ghawth,* who is always looking at Prophet ﷺ.

These characteristics of the *'abdāl* are important to understand, how *awlīyāullāh* interact and react. Some people like stories and some like something else, but since we entered this ocean, we have to finish it.

The characteristics Allāh ﷻ gave them is from the inner circle of *'abdāl,* as the *'abdāl* range in number—some *aḥadīth* say they are forty, some say seven. The highest level of *'abdāl* travel from their places, leaving behind their bodies, taking out from their bodies another copy, and they travel *dunyā* looking for people that need help and they help them. That is why when you see a *walī* who looks like they are sleeping, their soul left their body. In that state, don't wake them up, otherwise you will make a mistake, unless they instruct you, "Wake us up at that moment." That means you are calling them back; when they tell you, "Wake us up," it means, "Call us back;" then you are like an alarm for them, but if they don't say anything to you, don't wake them up.

I saw this with Grandshaykh ق and Mawlana Shaykh Nazim ق. One time I was passing by the window of Grandshaykh's ق room, going where there was *dhikr* and a window. One self was telling me to look and one self was telling me not to look, because when you witness certain things you cannot control yourself, but if you don't look you miss the opportunity.

So I looked and I saw Grandshaykh ق sitting like that and opening his mouth. And I was shocked to see that, you know on cold days when you go out and you blow and you see fog coming out? What was coming out was light. And from his head a greenish color and from his mouth, white color was coming up and they were mixing, like a rainbow. The whole ceiling disappeared and you saw it going up through this universe until you cannot see it anymore. And at that moment I was shaking.

"Why are you looking at something that does not belong to you? Run from here." *Alḥamdulillāh* I took the opportunity to see that, I didn't miss it. Keep him supporting us, *yā Rabb,* and give Mawlana Shaykh long life.

So when you see *awlīyāullāh* on the bed or floor or chair as if they are laying down sleeping, don't touch them or wake them up as they are not present there. For seven days Grandshaykh ق in seclusion left his body and went when Sayyīdinā Shah Naqshband ق appeared to him in a vision in *khalwah.* He left his body for seven days, no movement.

And his wife ran to Grandshaykh Sharafuddīn ق, Grandshaykh's uncle, and said, "ʿAbdAllāh Effendi died."

He said, "No, he didn't die. Leave him, he will be back in seven days."

Awlīyā have that power. If they tell you, accept. If they don't tell you, you are free to do what you like. But *al-amru fawq al-adab,* "the order is above good manners." If it is good manners not to drink from a cup, and if Shaykh tells you "drink", you do it. Don't say, "O Shaykh, it is your cup, it is not my cup." If the shaykh says go to this place, you go. Don't say, "I don't." Go! That is an order above good manners. In his heart it is higher than what you are thinking. There is wisdom to do that. And that is why you see them and always they know if there are objections. And

Grandshaykh ق said, bless his soul, "I never give an order except to two of my students. He used to say Nazim Effendi, Ḥusayn Effendi. They never have doubts. When Shaykh gives you an order, don't try to balance it in your balance. Don't say, "I have this, that, busy here or busy there." No, do it. One day he said to me, "I want you to take me downtown in the car." Grandshaykh ق. And it was a very new car. I will cut the story short. Would you like to hear it? (Yes, sir.) I said it before, where did I say it?

Alḥamdulillāh, my elder brother and my father liked to drive cars and so always we had the latest cars, ten cars. And every year we had new cars. One year we bought a very fancy car, very expensive, a sports car, and it was a Jaguar. And my brother and I said, "Let's go to visit Mawlana in this car." So we arrived and went up to visit him.

He said, "Today I like to go with you to the market, so you take me down."

We said, "OK." So we were happy, since it was a fancy car, and it was a small car, a sports car.

He came down and said, "What is this? This is garbage. Do you think this is a car? Naqshbandis must have the best. Change it, go get a big car."

So we went down to the market and it was small.

He said, "I want to buy wood."

You know, they cut the wood there and sold it. So Mawlana Shaykh filled the car with wood and all the dirt that comes from the wood was coming in the small trunk and on one of the seats.

And he said, "Next time don't come with that car, bring a big car." He was teaching, "Don't have love of *dunyā* in your heart."

Now, according to our minds, this was the best car. But he was giving to our mind that *dunyā* must not be *akbar hamminā,* most of our attention. So the next time, our father bought a Lincoln Continental, a big car with beige seats.

We said, "*Alḥamdulillāh,* we will take this car." We went to Syria.

Grandshaykh ق said, "*Yā awlād,* I want to go buy something from the market." So we took him in that car and he said, "This is a car for the Naqshbandi." So they like students to be the best. If you are poor, no problem, but act and speak the best, then people will see this *ṭarīqah* as something great.

Don't look poor! That means don't look poor in your appearance, look rich, *mutaḥammis,* to have zeal, *yazal,* showing that you are great with this *ṭarīqah,* that you are not a stinky person, a poor person in your manners. Have rich manners: accept and not deny, give and not be greedy, love and extend your hand to everyone! Even if you receive from others what you don't like, don't give it back.

Keep good relationships. For seven years Prophet ﷺ had a neighbor throwing garbage on his door, and he never complained. Every morning at *Fajr* time, he saw the garbage and he took the garbage and didn't tell anyone. And finally that neighbor was dying, after seven years and he went to see him. And that neighbor said, "O *Rasūlullāh,* seven years I am giving you a hard time. If this is Islam, then I accept Islam." That is the teaching of *awlīyāullāh.*

So we took Grandshaykh ق and he said, "Take me to the charcoal market." There are two kinds of charcoal, the wood one, the long one, and there is the coal from inside the ground, which has a lot of dust. He bought bags of charcoal and said to the merchant, "Put it in the trunk," and that trunk became dusty black. And that was not enough; he put charcoal on the seats and he beige, clean color became all-black. And he was happy, looking at us to see what we were going to say. What you can say? And so they tell you, "Don't look at our actions; there is wisdom in it." It means don't make your heart dirty like charcoal dust; keep your heart clean." If they say, "Do this," do it. "Don't do this," don't do it. Then you will be successful.

We will continue later. May Allāh ﷻ forgive us and keep us under the mercy of His Prophet, Sayyīdinā Muḥammad ﷺ, and under Allāh's mercy, and the mercy of *awlīyāullāh*. Without that we are lost.

Who Are the People of Islam?

Sayyīdinā Muḥammad al-Busayrī ق said, *Tūba lana ma'ashar-Islāmi inna lana min al-ināyati ruknan ghayra munhadim,* "Good tidings for us, the People of Islam!"

He ﷺ said, *ma'ashar al-Islām,* "People of Islam", not, *ma'ashar al-muslimīn,* "Muslims". It means People of Islam are those who accept Islam with its perfection. Muslims are not in perfection, so Muslims are not in good tidings; rather, those who are perfecting their Islam have good tidings. Those who are not perfecting their Islam, who backbite, do not receive good tidings. He said, "Good tidings to the People of Islam. *Inna lana min al-inayāti,* "Allāh ﷻ granted us from His endless blessing a supporting pole that is never falling down." That means the Prophet ﷺ.

O Muslims! As Mawlana says, O Attenders! If we lose love of *Āhlu 'l-Bayt,* then we lose love of Prophet Muḥammad ﷺ, as it says in Holy Qur'an:

Qul lā asalukum 'alayhi ajran illa 'l-māwaddata fi 'l-qurbā.
Say, "No reward do I ask of you for this except the love of those near of kin."
(Sūrat ash-Shūrā', 42:23)

Say, O Muḥammad, "I am not asking any return for what *dawa* I am delivering to you. I am not asking anything, I will give you everything. But I only ask one thing: love my family. Keep *wud,* compassion, emotions, love for my family."

Where is love for Prophet's family today? Where are you, Ahl as-Sunnah wal-Jama'ah, showing love to Prophet's family? That is what we are ordered to do. Allāh is saying in Holy Qur'an, *Qul lā asalukum 'alayhi ajran illa 'l-māwaddata fi 'l-qurbā.* "I am not asking anything for what I do for you, but to love my family and care for them," to the Day of Judgment. Are you looking? Where are *Āhlu 'l-Bayt*? Write his name, write his email, and make a collection of *Āhlu 'l-Bayti* families. There must be millions in this time from *Āhlu 'l-Bayt*! Do you have a relationship with them?

That is what Prophet ﷺ is asking, "I am asking only to keep love to them." That means you must look for them, and especially some *Āhlu 'l-Bayt* who are *awlīyāullāh*. Do you look for them?

And that is our message: Allāh ﷻ put *awlīyāullāh* everywhere in the world to guide us to *Āhlu 'l-Bayt*, to see them and to take *barakah* from them. Most, if not all *awlīyāullāh* are from *Āhlu 'l-Bayt*. Look at Sayyīdinā Salman al-Farsi ؓ, who is not from the blood of Prophet ﷺ, but whom Prophet made to be from his family because of his love for him, and they considered him to be from *Āhlu 'l-Bayt*.

Prophet ﷺ left an authentic *hadīth*, "I am leaving behind two things, that you never lose the way: *kitābullāh*, the Book of Allāh, and *ʿitratī*, my family." He put his family up with the Book of Allāh. Look after *Āhlu 'l-Bayt*. If you are really *ʿulamā* you know that He honored them to be from *Āhlu 'l-Bayt*. Not everyone is from *Āhlu 'l-Bayt*. Allāh ﷻ gave them that love from Prophet ﷺ, and everyone has to respect them. May Allāh ﷻ give us the respect that is needed for *Āhlu 'l-Bayt*.

May Allāh ﷻ forgive us and may Allāh ﷻ bless us.

Wa min Allāhi 't-tawfiq, bi ḥurmati 'l-ḥabīb, bi ḥurmati 'l-Fātiḥah.
And with Allāh is success. For the sake of the Beloved, for his sake we recite the opening chapter of Holy Qur'an.

Knowledge of Taste and Knowledge of Papers

Aʿūdhu billāhi min ash-Shayṭāni 'r-rajīm. Bismillāhi' r-Raḥmāni 'r-Raḥīm. Nawaytu 'l-arbāʿīn, nawaytu 'l-ʿitikāf, nawaytu'l-khalwah, nawaytu 'l-ʿuzlah, nawaytu 'r-riyāḍa, nawaytu 's-sulūk, lillāhi Taʿalā fī hādhā 'l-masjid. Atīʿūllāha wa atīʿū 'r-Rasūla wa ūli 'l-amri minkum. (4:59)

M*an dhāqa ẓafar, wa man lam yudhiq khasir,* "Who tastes will succeed or win, and who does not taste will lose, and between succeeding and losing there is no description and no resemblance." The one who succeeds will know the purity and the taste of that food. The one who is not tasking is like a patient who has lost taste in his mouth. Whatever you give him of the best food or grass, it is the same.

If you give grass to the one who has the ability to taste, he will not take it, he will say, "No, give me the best of what you have. I am looking at your generosity, give me from the best." The other one is sick, a patient, so whatever you give him he will take, because he just wants to fill his stomach as he has no taste. It is like feeding someone by a stomach tube to keep him alive. But the one you are feeding through the mouth is far better, because he has the sense of taste and he will appreciate what Allāh gave him.

Awlīyāullāh are the ones who have taste. For those who are not reaching that level, it is very difficult to explain it to them because they don't feel it. It only becomes like *ʿIlm al-Awrāq,* Knowledge of Papers, with no more knowledge of taste. And not everyone can reach *ʿIlm al-Adhwāq,* Knowledge of Taste, because there is a problem within us that we are not able to overcome: we allow our ego ride us. However, *awlīyāullāh* are able to ride their egos. Allāh said in Holy Qur'an:

> *Wa aʿaida lahum mastaṭaʿtum min quwwatin wa min ribāṭ al-khayli turhibūna bihi ʿadūwuallāhi wa ʿadūwakum.*
>
> *And prepare against them all you can of power, including steeds of war, to strike terror into (the hearts of) the enemies of Allāh and your enemies.*
>
> (Sūrat al-'Anfāl, 8:60)

Electricity has power that if you touch, you can faint or maybe die. Power is a strong support that Allāh is sending to us. When Allāh is saying, "Prepare for them power," that means power to make your enemy faint or be killed. When Allāh orders something, it means he is giving support for that and the support is there. *Awlīyāullāh* take that support, not accepting their own power, but to take from Allāh's Ocean of Power, *Baḥr al-Qudrah.* When they take from there, they are supported against their Shayṭān who keeps running after everyone. Prophet ﷺ said, "I am the only one on earth that *aslāmtu* Shayṭān, I made my Shayṭān surrender to me."

Who is the biggest enemy to Prophet ﷺ? It is the one who refused to make *sajda.* When Allāh ordered angels to make *sajda* to Adam ﷺ; he refused due to seeing that light of Muḥammad ﷺ in Adam's forehead. Out of jealousy he refused, claiming, "Why he has to take *Maqām al-Maḥmūd* and not me?" and so Allāh cursed him. Prophet said, "I made my Shayṭān surrender." That means, "I made Iblīs surrender to me." It means, "O Iblīs! You have to know I am Muḥammad; Allāh gave me *Maqām al-Maḥmūd,* and He sent me as a mercy to humanity! As much you run after people of my *ummah,* they are mine and you will not succeed because the *ummah* is for me! Whatever you make them do, I am taking them to Paradise." For sure Prophet ﷺ will not allow that anyone will go without *shafāʿa.* He said:

Shafaʿatī li ahl al-kabā'ir min ummatī.
My intercession is for the big sinners of my nation. (Tirmidhī)

This means the small sinners are already included, because all of us do sin. Although Allāh gave Prophet *shafāʿa* and he will take the *ummah* with him to Paradise, we must still struggle to make our Shayṭān surrender, we must not leave it loose. Don't leave your horse loose. You cannot hold the horse, you have to keep the reins in your hands. Allāh ﷻ said:

Wa aʿidda lahum mastaṭaʿtum min quwwah.
Against them make ready your strength to the utmost of your power.

"Whatever you can prepare, whatever you are able to, do it!" That means Allāh will not burden you with more than you can carry. Allāh is "al-Ghafūr" and "*Arhamu 'r-rāhimīn.*" Whatever you can do, struggle against Shayṭān! People are not your enemy. Today they say, "This country is an enemy to us." They want to make enmity.

Wa jazāu sayyi'atin sayyi'atun mithluhā faman 'afā wa aslaha fa-ajruhu 'alā Allāh. innahu lā yuhibbu 'z-zālimīn.
The recompense for an evil is an evil like thereof, but whoever forgives and makes reconciliation, his reward is due from Allāh. Verily, He likes not the oppressors. (Sūrat ash-Shūrā', 42:40)

Why make enemies? If I make a rocket, you make a rocket. If I make an atomic bomb, you make an atomic bomb. For what? This is arrogance, to say, "I am stronger than you and I want you to be under my feet." In this way they create enmity. Allāh ﷻ is telling you your enemy is Shayṭān, no one else. So if you want to succeed, prepare whatever power you can for that struggle. It is like struggling to start a car in winter. You want to run it, but on cold days it doesn't start. You try and try, and then after a while, it starts. You keep trying until the battery finishes. Allāh is saying to keep struggling until your battery is finished; then you have surrendered to Allāh ﷻ. Don't lose hope! Allāh said, *min ribāṭi 'l-khayl,* "prepare reins." He didn't say, "Prepare horses only." You need a horse to fight your enemy, which means you need a vehicle.

O Muslims! You have to know that every word in the Holy Qur'an has a meaning; not the meaning that comes to your mind, but thousands of meanings! He told you to prepare your power and then prepare your vehicles, horses. You must prepare your reins. How do you control that horse? You need a vehicle that will take you wherever you are going and which is under a command. In a car you have brake, whether it is a stick shift or automatic. You have everything on an airplane to make sure you are running it well. You cannot run a car without a steering wheel. Allāh is saying that you have to prepare horses, but you have to be ready with reins.

And the example of that is, one of the *awlīyāullāh,* Sayyīdinā Abāyazīd al-Bistāmī ق, who reached a highest level in his time. He was able to hear heavenly voices coming. He was in the *Ka'bah* holding the round chain that opens the door to the *Ka'bah,* saying, "*Yā Rabbī*! Give me permission, only five minutes to catch Iblīs. I will catch him and chain him so that he cannot run after *Ummat an-Nabī.*" One *walī* has that power, so what do you think of other *awlīyā*? Allāh gave them power as they prepared themselves.

A voice came to his heart, "*Yā* Bayāzīd, why are you asking? Do you think I cannot stop Iblīs? Without a second or a moment, with no time, if My Will comes to stop it, immediately he is melted! He will disappear from this universe. *Yā* Bayāzīd! Look up above you at the *multazam,* at the door of *Kaʿbah."*

He looked up and fainted. Allāh left him in that state, and after a while he came back to normal, and began to crawl around the *Kaʿbah* saying, "*Yā Rabbī ʿafwak wa riḍāk,* Your forgiveness and Your mercy! I made a mistake to interfere in Your Will. I am asking forgiveness."

Allāh ﷻ said, "*Yā* Bayāzīd! What you saw is My manifestation of My mercy descending on My House."

> *Ṭāhhir baytī li 'ṭ-ṭā'ifīn wa 'l-ʿakifīn wa 'r-rukaʿi 's-sujūd.*
> *That they should sanctify My House for those who compass it round, or use it as a retreat, or bow, or prostrate themselves (therein in prayer).*
>
> (Sūrat al-Baqarah, 2:125)

"I am sending that mercy on my House. *Yā* Bayāzīd! If you catch Iblīs that means no one is going to struggle, and I give My mercy to those who are struggling. If there is no Shayṭān, it is as if people are living in Paradise, then all are on the same level. But I let them struggle to manifest on them My mercy. And when My mercy is manifested, those who receive more are more near, those who receive less are farther away."

That is why *awlīyāullāh* are able to prepare that power, that possibility of, "prepare your power". Sometimes you see on a remote control or in cars, or anywhere else, a button labeled "power". If you don't press that button, nothing works, although you continue to play with the remote. Press the power button and all the other buttons will work, even thousands of buttons. Look at a space shuttle, how many thousands of buttons it has? But they need one button in the beginning. If you open that one button, then everything opens to you and then you can taste everything. There is a button with 10 watts or 20 watts, or 30, 240, 360, 1,000 volts, 10 megavolts, or 100 megavolts; it depends on how strong your button is.

Allāh ﷻ said, "O Bayāzīd! However much I am sending and people are taking by struggling against their egos and purifying themselves, they are going to receive that *raḥmāh!"*

Why Allāh sent *Ummat an-Nabī* or all of humanity to circumambulate His House? Why do we have to go there to circumambulate, are we going to circumambulate the walls? What is inside? Some people go inside, and they find it just like the outside. The inside is not visible, it is like an X-ray, not visible to your eyes but visible to the eyes of the machine. Are the eyes of a machine better than your eyes? No. So why can't our eyes see, and the eyes of the machine can? Because the button for our eyes is not pressed. You press the button on the machine to give it power. *Awlīyāullāh* have pressed that button already.

That is why they are explaining about those five different types of *awlīyā* and the many different groups. But all of them come under a leader, as all prophets come under the Seal of Messengers, Sayyīdinā Muḥammad ﷺ. All *awlīyā* come under the *Ghawth*, who inherits from the heart of Prophet. His button is huge, and under him are the five *quṭbs*, and under them are five groups of *awlīyāullāh*. We mentioned the five *quṭbs:* Quṭb, Quṭb al-Bilād, Quṭb al-Mutaṣarrif, Quṭb al-Irshād, and Quṭb al-Aqtāb. And under each there are five groups and under them, there might be up to 70,000 *awlīyā*. Under each *quṭb* there is a head of each group; head of Budalā, head of Nujabā, head of Nuqabā, head of Awtād, and head of Akhyār. And under each of them come 70,000 *awlīyā* that are spread out, and all have power buttons. Some have more, some have less. They have prepared themselves, they have that power.

But without a vehicle you cannot move; their guides as their vehicle. That is why it is very important to have a vehicle. You need to have *quwwah, wa aʿidda lahum,* and He added on that *wa min ribāṭi 'l-khayl,* "from reins of horses." That means you need a vehicle with reins that takes you to safety. *Turhibūn bihi ʿ adūwullāh wa ʿadūwakum,* "(You will) strike terror into (the hearts of) the enemies, of Allāh and your enemies." Who is Allāh's enemy? Allāh's enemy is Iblīs. And who are human beings' enemies? They are devils and evil *shayṭāns,* and Iblīs. How do you terrorize them? By not listening to them; then they become upset with you and come more heavy on you. That is what happened with Sayyīdinā Abū Yazīd al-Bistāmi ق.

One time he was visiting Madinah al-Munawwarah, the *maqām* of Prophet ﷺ, and it was raining heavily. He saw someone holding a lot of reins and passing them to people who were also there to visit. He was putting a rein on every one's mouth. Abū Yazīd ق looked at him with a normal look; he is a man, giving them reins like we put on horses. Then he looked with heavenly power and saw that is Iblīs. There is a place in everyone's heart where he can enter. *Thumma āmanū, thumma kafarū.* One time we are in belief, one time we are in unbelief; one leg here, one leg there. We hope we are always on the good side and for when we are on the bad side, we hope Allāh forgives us.

Abū Yazīd ق said, "Do you have reins for me?"

Iblīs replied, "O Bayāzīd! For all of these I have reins, but you I will ride without reins!"

For that one moment of heedlessness, it came. *Awlīyāullāh* are not *ma'sūm* (innocent) like prophets. One moment made him fall.

He said, "I don't need reins to ride you, these are easy."

And Abū Yazīd ق cursed him saying, "O you *mal'ūn*!"

For the next few days it rained constantly. You know the Earth there doesn't swallow rain water for the benefit of people, to make streams to run. Madinah was flooded, water was coming up to the necks of people. I saw that one time in Mecca. Entire Mecca was flooded and in the *Ka'bah* water reached to your neck. This was when we were doing *ṭawāf* with Mawlana Shaykh Nazim ق in 1979. We did the first *ṭawāf*, then the second, the third, and at the beginning of the fourth *tawaf*, Shaykh Nazim ق stopped.

He raised his hands and said, "O Allāh! We are coming all the way here. Send us Your mercy, send us the rain." And he made a *du'ā* that I had never heard before, a very strong one. When he finished his *du'ā* we began the fourth *ṭawāf*. As soon as we passed Hajar al-Aswad, clouds came from everywhere, formed a thunderstorm, and it began to rain. There was no possibility for the rain water to drain. The *Ka'bah* was filling up, the Ḥarām filled with water up to our necks. I experienced that.

So when the water filled up in Madinah, Abū Yazīd ق saw an old man in trouble, and he asked that one, O! May I help you?"

He said, "I have to cross from here to there."

So Abū Yazīd ق said, "Okay, I will carry you," and he climbed on Abū Yazīd's back.

When they reached the other side and Abū Yazīd helped him to dry ground, that one turned smiling and said, "You see Abū Yazīd! I told you I will ride you without reins!"

From one moment of heedlessness he had to pay that big invoice, that big price. Allāh ﷻ gave *awlīyāullāh* that power to prepare their strength in order to defeat Shayṭān for the benefit of the *ummah*. That is what we were describing yesterday, the Budalā, the first of these *awlīyā* after *quṭbs*. There are too many powers, spiritual and physical, that we explained some yesterday. This is an abbreviation between two brackets, only to understand that we are explaining, reading, or teaching from papers, but Mawlana wants us to taste what he wants to say. It is very hard to understand how these *awlīyā* work. So now between the brackets there is an insert to show you that there are such men to whom Allāh gave authority for the benefit of all humanity.

May Allāh ﷻ forgive us and bless us.

Wa min Allāhi 't-tawfiq, bi ḥurmati 'l-ḥabīb, bi ḥurmati 'l-Fātiḥah.
And with Allāh is success. For the sake of the Beloved, for his sake we recite the opening chapter of Holy Qur'an.

Saints Dwell in What Allah Likes

A'ūdhu billāhi min ash-Shayṭāni 'r-rajīm. Bismillāhi' r-Raḥmāni 'r-Raḥīm. Nawaytu 'l-arbā'īn, nawaytu 'l-'itikāf, nawaytu'l-khalwah, nawaytu 'l-'uzlah, nawaytu 'r-riyāḍa, nawaytu 's-sulūk, lillāhi Ta'alā fī hādhā 'l-masjid. Atī'ūllāha wa atī'ū 'r-Rasūla wa ūli 'l-amri minkum. (4:59)

Two or three days ago, Mawlana Shaykh gave a *ṣuḥbah* in which he said, "I have to go down to that level so we can learn where we are standing. However high you think of yourself, you are never going to see yourself higher than a president or a king of a country." He said, "O presidents, O kings of countries! Where do you think you are flying?"

There is nothing higher than that in *dunyā,* in the ego realm. This is important for us to learn, to understand later what are the meanings of the various levels and ranks, and I will repeat them another time. There is the level *"Ghawth"*, and under him the five *quṭbs*: Quṭb, Quṭb al-Bilād, Quṭb al-Aqtāb, Quṭb al-Irshād, and Quṭb al-Mutaṣarrif. Under every one of these there are the five different groups of *awlīyā;* Budalā, Nujabā, Nuqabā, Awtād, and Akhyār.

It is difficult to understand their levels or what they do, because if we meet one of them, we see something of *mughayyar at-tafkīr,* contrary to what we think. You think this way, that is correct, but that *walī* is acting differently and you protest, complain, and sometimes you run away and say, "What is he doing?" You don't know; it might be a test for you.

Allāh ﷻ gave a big example in Holy Qur'an of Sayyīdinā Mūsā ﷺ, who came with Sharī'ah, the heavenly constitution. Allāh sent him to one of His servants, Sayyīdinā Khiḍr ﷺ, to whom He gave a different kind of knowledge, and Sayyīdinā Mūsā was not able to keep patience with that one. *innaka lan tastaṭi' ma'īya sabra.* He (Khiḍr) said to him (Mūsā), "You cannot be patient with me." If he was patient, the knowledge would have opened up, but Allāh wants us to learn, so He used this as an example for us.

To go along with someone to whom Allāh ﷻ has given a knowledge different from yours, you will not meet (come to terms), because their knowledge is the destruction of the ego: they want to destroy your ego and kill it. So what did Sayyīdinā Khiḍr ﷺ do first?

Fantalaqā ḥattā idhā rakiba fi 's-safinati kharaqahā. Qāla akharaqtahā li tughriqa āhlahā. Laqad ji'ta shayan imrā.
So the two set out until, when they were in the ship, he made a hole in it. (Moses) said, "Have you made a hole to drown the folk therein? Verily you have done a dreadful thing!" (Sūrat al-Kahf, 18:71)

When they went on the boat, what did he do? *Allāhu Akbar*! He made a hole. It might be that he had some kind of drill at that time, so he drilled it. How did he make the hole? It didn't mention in Holy Qur'an that he had equipment. If there was equipment, it was a very old kind of equipment and it would take a long time to make a hole. But with the heavenly power Allāh ﷻ gave to him, *wa ʿalamnāhu min ladunna ʿilma,* "We have taught him from heavenly knowledge." (18:65) By looking, he made a hole. So what happened? *Qāla akharaqtahā li tughriqa āhlahā,* Sayyīdinā Mūsā ﷺ asked, "Did you make a hole in order to make it sink and drown the people within it?" Of course, that is the Boat of Safety. What is the boat? It is to take you from a shore to another shore. But that vehicle you went on is your ego. That is why *awlīyā* want to make a hole in your ego. They want to suck away your ego, to throw it out and then you don't need it anymore. Even if there are hundreds of holes, the body will fly, as when Sayyīdinā Jalāluddin ar-Rumi ق was whirling, he was rising and was lifted up as gravity was no longer able to pull him down.

Sayyīdinā Mūsā was unable to accept that hole, and he complained. Sayyīdinā Khiḍr said, "I told you, you are not patient." How did Allāh ﷻ give Sayyīdinā Khiḍr, *al-jassāra ḥattā yukhāṭib Mūsā bi hadha 'l-khiṭāb*? He gave him that bravery or courage to speak like that to Sayyīdinā Mūsā, who is *ūlū 'l-ʿazam,* one of the Five Highest Prophets. Sayyīdinā Khiḍr must be bowing to Sayyīdinā Mūsā, giving respect and honor to Sayyīdinā Mūsā. But Allāh ﷻ gave him that courage to teach, not Sayyīdinā Mūsā, because it may be Sayyīdinā Mūsā was hiding his reality from Sayyīdinā Khiḍr to teach us, so we may learn.

He said, "Why did you do that?"

So Khiḍr said, "I told you, you will not be patient with me! Wait for the second step."

That first incident is easy. The second one was, they left the boat and it was sinking, sinking, sinking. When they reached the other shore, Sayyīdinā Khiḍr killed a boy.

F'anṭalaqa ḥattā idhā laqīya ghulāman fa qatalahu qāla aqtalta nafsan zakīyyatan bi ghayri nafsin laqad j'ita shayan nukrā.

Then they proceeded until, when they met a young man, he slew him. Moses said, "Have you slain an innocent person who had slain none? Truly a foul (unheard of) thing you have done!" (Sūrat al-Kahf, 18:74)

Sayyīdinā Mūsā ☙ said, "How? First we understand the boat, but now you are killing someone who did no sin."

Sayyīdinā Khiḍr ☙ repeated, "I told you that you are not going to be patient with me."

That is why it is very difficult to go along with these *awlīyāullāh*. Yesterday they were telling me there were viewers on Sufilive who could not go along. They love the shaykh, but they said, "We see things around the shaykh that we don't understand." They are around the shaykh but cannot understand how he does not object. He is in complete submission to Allāh's will, whatever Allah put for him. For such people, whatever comes or goes, they submit.

People cannot accept or understand, so they complain. But they have to know that the *walī's* knowledge is not equal to the knowledge of normal people. If Allāh ☙ doesn't give you that knowledge, you cannot understand the work of someone who has that knowledge. It is like what happened with Sayyīdinā Mūsā ☙, who is not a normal person—he is a prophet and a messenger—but Allāh ☙ didn't give him that knowledge, to show him, "What I give you, I give you. What I give someone else, don't try to ask about it."

And then Khiḍr did the third thing for Mūsā.

F'anṭalaqa ḥattā idhā ātayā āhla qaryatin istaṭ'amā āhlahā fa abaw an yuḍayyifūhumā fawajadā fīhā jidāran yurīdu an yanqaḍḍa fa aqāmahu qāla law sh'ita lattakhadhta 'alayhi ajrā.

Then they proceeded until, when they came to the inhabitants of a town, they asked them for food, but they refused them hospitality. They found there a wall on the point of falling down, but he set it up straight. (Moses) said, "If you had wished, surely you could have exacted some recompense for it!"

(Sūrat al-Kahf, 18:77)

The third incident was, they entered a village and saw a wall completely falling apart and the treasure that was under it was going to be exposed. So Sayyīdinā Khiḍr ☙ immediately restored the wall, although when they entered they asked people to host them and they refused. This means that when someone harms you, return it with goodness. And Sayyīdinā Mūsā ﷺ, in his Sharīʿah, constitution, it is written, *Al-ʿayn bi 'l-ʿayn,* "An eye for an eye." If someone pokes your eye, you poke his eye. *Wa 's-sin bi 's-sin,* "and a tooth for a tooth." If someone broke your tooth, you break his tooth. In another Sharīʿah of Sayyīdinā ʿĪsā ﷺ, whoever hits you on your right cheek, turn the left for him to hit.

In the Sharīʿah of Prophet ﷺ, the highest level of *iḥsān* is to submit. If they hit you, don't move, because when you turn, as Sayyīdinā ʿĪsā ﷺ said, "When they hit you on your right, turn for them your left," ego is there. It is saying, "I am better than you. You are hitting me on my right, and I am turning for you my left, beat me also." There is some kind of egoism there. But in the *Maqām al-Iḥsān* as taught by Prophet, you submit. They beat you on the right, they beat you on the left, they beat you on the head, wherever they beat you, you are submitting.

To understand *awlīyāullāh* is very difficult. But we are giving these examples so that even if we can't explain, at least we can understand their powers. So Mawlana Shaykh Nazim ق said, "O presidents and kings! I am sorry to say this," and I am quoting, "but I have to say it. You are sitting in your big palaces and sometimes meeting other presidents. And then a bell is ringing. What do you do? You leave the important session entirely and run, responding to that bell. Because that place is calling you, 'Come, come to me, I am waiting. I love you. I want to see you there. I cannot be without you. Leave your palace and come to my toilet quickly!' So you leave your palace and go down to that place." Especially if you have a bad stomach, it keeps ringing and you might cancel all your meetings!

Allāh is showing no matter how you can be the highest, don't think you are the highest. "I made you to be in need for the lowest." Don't see your ego. *Awlīyāullāh* don't like you to *as-simaʿ*, listen to your ego or to something coming out of your ego; they want you to listen only to what Allāh and His Prophet are ordering you.

Man yuṭiʿi 'r-rasūla faqad atāʿullāh.
Whoever obeys the Prophet obeys Allāh. (Sūrat an-Nisa, 4:80)

Mā atākumu 'r-rasūl fakhudhūhu wa mā nahākum ʿanhu fantahū.
Leave what Prophet forbade and take what he ordered. (Sūrat al-Hashr, 59:7)

So, in order to understand, Imām Shādhilī ق said, *alfaw ābāuhum ḍāllīn,* "They followed traces and footsteps of their ancestors who are on the wrong way." Don't follow their footsteps or their traces, they are *ḍāllīn,* "on the wrong path;" they deviated from the right path. Prophet ﷺ said, "We are, *naḥnu ummatan wasaṭan,* a moderate nation, in the middle, not on the two extremes." We are not on the right side too much and not on the left side too much, but in the middle. We are not so liberal; we have to know our limits. Know your limits, like in a country you have laws and you have to know your limits, you cannot trespass them.

Why do some people say, "You have to be liberal, if you are liberal your Islam is good." No, that is not correct. You are liberal in the meaning of what Islam is giving you, in the knowledge of the constitution. And you are liberal in the meaning of what your country's constitution is. You cannot trespass against it. Can you trespass against the police and say, "I don't want to give my ID or my driver's license." What will happen? You will go to jail. If the police say, "Give me your ID," what do you say? "Yes, sir! This is my ID." Be moderate. Don't say, "no," or you will end up in jail.

Awlīyāullāh look at you and they know what is your ID. If they say, "Give us your ID," you don't say, "no." This means you have to submit. When you don't submit to your shaykh, you're finished. Even if you do whatever you like to do, you cannot be raised up. *Al-amru fawqu 'l-adab. Amr,* the order of the shaykh, is above your knowledge, even if you are the biggest scholar. How a scholar of Islam, those who knew that matter, came to the *shuyūkh* and it might be that the shaykh is not on the academic level of the scholar, but he is a *walī* in spiritual, heavenly knowledge, which is better. You have to surrender to him even if you are the biggest scholar and you know everything. No, you know everything by *awrāq,* papers, but you don't know everything by taste. Taste is different. Even if he gives you a small sip of taste, any, it is enough for you to save you on the Day of Judgment, because he gave you something that refreshed your body Today they say an "energy pill" gives you energy.

So Imām Shādhilī ق said, "Don't follow your ancestors who deviated; if they were wrong, don't follow them."

Innahum alfaw ābā'ahum ḍāllīna fahum ʿalā 'āthārihim yuhraʿūn.
Verily, they found their fathers on the wrong path, so they (too) made haste to follow in their footsteps! (Sūrat aṣ-Ṣaffāt, 37:69,70)

They followed the footsteps of their ancestors, but they were wrong. But as we said, when the *walī* gives you an order, the *walī* is above your decisions and knowledge, so even if you think it is wrong, you must do it.

Of course Sayyīdinā Khiḍr knew you cannot make a hole in a boat. But he made a hole, as there was wisdom in saving that boat from the king who was a tyrant. He was taking the boat of every poor person. Allāh didn't show that knowledge to Sayyīdinā Mūsā, but showed it to Khiḍr. So when they asked Imām Shādhilī ق about *sim'a,* hearing, he said, "Be careful of what your ego wants you to hear. Only hear what Allāh wants you to hear. Ego likes you to hear itself and it doesn't allow you to hear what Allāh wants."

And he said, *rā'ita bi 'l-manām ka-annī bayna yadayya kitāb al-faqīh ibn 'abd as-salām. wa fī yadihi 'l-yusrā awrāqan min ash-sha'r. fa tanāwala ustādhī al-kitābayn minnī wa qāla lī ka 'l-mustahzī ata'dilūna 'ani 'l-'ilm az-zakīyya,* "I saw in a dream, as if between my hands is the book of one of the famous scholars, al-'Izz Ibn 'Abd as-Salām. And in the left hand, *awrāqan min ash-sha'r,* 'papers of poetry.' One is a book of a very scholarly *walī*; he is a scholar and a *walī* at the same time. And in the left hand is a book or papers of poetry."

Today they study Sayyīdinā Jalāluddin Rumi's ق poetry. Do they know more than that? They explain but do not understand the taste of his knowledge; they read it as poetry.

Imām Shādhilī ق continues, "I saw my teacher standing and saying, *fa tanāwala kitāba faqīhihi bi-yamīnihi wa awrāq sha'ar bi yassārih.* 'I saw the books of Abdus-Salām in his right hand and in his left hand, a book of poetry. And he said sarcastically, *ata'dilūna 'ani'l-'ilm az-zakīyya fa ashār ila awrāq ash-sha'r fa ramāhā fi'l-arḍ,* "Are you balancing? What kind of value are you giving? Do you prefer the poetry over the scholarly writings of that *faqīh*?" And he took the poetry and threw the papers on the floor. He said, *fa man akthar min hadha fa-hūwa 'abda hawwāhu wa asīru shahwatahu wa munāhu,* 'Who will give more attention to these papers of poetry, (opposed to the real knowledge of *awlīyāullāh), fahuw 'abdun marqūqan li 'l-hawwā,* he is slave of his desires, *wa asīran li shahwatih,* and he is a prisoner to his bad desires and he is also a prisoner to what is *munā,* something that is good, but he became a prisoner to that arrogance or pride of that kind of knowledge that is in poetry.' And he said, *yastariqūn qulūb al-juhalā,* 'This poetry is only to attract the hearts of heedless people.'"

When they write these songs and sing them, it is not in Allāh's Way. It is describing *dunyā* and making all children, youth, and adults run to it. They don't listen to Imām al-Busayrī ق, they say it is *bid'a*. When someone is describing Prophet ﷺ and something heavenly, they say, "That is *bid'a*." They run after their desires.

Imām Shādhilī ق continues, "They have no will to do goodness or to reach Gnosticism. They will never reach what the People of Vision will reach." *Allāhu Akbar*! They sway when they hear Shakespeare. You see how they go and dance, especially to songs of Hollywood and the Middle East. There are more cable stations now for Arabic popular music than stations teaching *irfān*, Gnosticism, real spirituality!

Allah Wants You to Be for Him Only

They are only listening, and they think what satisfies their egos is all there is. But they are not able to visualize that what they are hearing is what Allāh wants. Allāh wants you only to hear *dhikrūllāh*. He wants you to hear only His Name and to be remembering Allāh and his Prophet ﷺ.

Alā bi dhikrūllāhi taṭma'inu 'l-qulūb.
In the remembrance of Allāh do hearts find satisfaction. (Sūrat ar-Ra'd, 13:28)

And that is what Grandshaykh ق is mentioning:

Wa ṭāhhir baytī li 'ṭ-ṭā'ifīn wa 'l-'akifīn wa 'r-ruka'i 's-sujūd.
And sanctify My House for those who compass it round, or stand up, or bow, or prostrate themselves (there in prayer). (Sūrat al-Ḥajj, 22:26)

Allāh has *ghīra,* possessiveness. He wants His servant to be for Him only, not for Iblīs or Shayṭān. He wants you to be only for Him! When Prophet ﷺ demonstrated he was for Him, Allāh raised him, calling him for *Mi'rāj*. He raised him by putting his name with His Name before all Creation, because He loves him. He doesn't want anyone to share that. What are we doing? We are running after ourselves and our desires and excitement. *Lā in lam yantahi ẓāliman lā,* "If that oppressor who does not follow the footsteps of Prophet ..."

*Qul in kuntum tuḥibbūn-Allāha fattabiʿūnī yuḥbibkumu Allāhu wa yaghfir
lakum dhunūbakum w'Allāhu ghafūrun Raḥīm.*
Say, "If you love Allāh, follow me (Muḥammad). Allāh will love you and
forgive you your sins, for Allāh is Oft-Forgiving, Most Merciful."

(Sūrat 'Āli 'Imrān, 3:31)

Don't listen to what is coming to your ear. You have to check, as you
are not yet ready. If you don't have a real shaykh but only a fake shaykh,
what comes to your ear might not be correct. A real shaykh can correct you
from far away and even fix your hearing. Allāh said if you are an oppressor,
not listening to what He likes, he will flip you upside-down. Heavens will
be Earth and your Earth will be Heavens.

He said, "No, it is not what you are explaining." See how the shaykh
interferes quickly. *idhā kānat ar-rū bi-amṭāri 'l-ʿulūmi dāratun wa 'n-nafs bi
ṣāliḥati nabātatun,* "If the soul has been showered with heavenly rain, the
rain of knowledge, it is going to be *dāratun,* like pearl, glowing and shining,
and whatever the ego is doing will come out from it, as when grass grows it
comes up and grows under the rain of that knowledge. That is okay. That is
why, with the knowledge that Allāh showered on Sayyīdinā Khiḍr 著, he
was under it. Whatever his *nafs* did, whatever he did, was okay. Although
he made a hole in the boat, killed the boy, and built the wall, it was okay.
Meaning he gave you a vehicle with a hole, it cannot reach anywhere. But
even if it has a hole, the way you are going has lots of holes and will make
all your good *ʿamal* disappear.

You must be careful. Then when you are careful, kill the boy (the ego).
And when you submit, *ʿallamnāhu min laddunna ʿilma.* When he stopped
Shayṭān from attacking the treasures of your heart, he made it safe for you
in a safety box so Shayṭān cannot touch it.

Therefore, if the showers on the soul are *dāratun,* showering you with
that knowledge, the soul will grow, and then the heavenly self will do what
is written according to Allāh's will. Then *thabat al-khayr kullih,* "Confirm
whatever you do."

But what if the self was successful, *wa 'r-rūḥu maghlūbatan,* and the soul
is defeated by the ego? That is why you have to be careful of what you listen
to. Today when they go to the music areas, they sway. So he said, *idhā kāna
an-nafs ghālibatun illa ḥasal al-qaḥṭ wa 'l-jadab,* "If the ego was successful, then
there will be no crops and there will be famine and drought." Everything
will be finished. Whatever you do will not be fruitful. *Fa anqaḍa al-amr wa jā
ash-sharr kullāhu,* "then the issue will be delivered and complete evil will

ensue. Therefore, we say *al-amr fawq al-adab*, do what they say." Don't say, "What is this or that?" Kill the boy, kill the boy!

Sayyīdinā Mūsā ﷺ is teaching *Ummat an-Nabī* that if you allow the soul to be conquered, all of your affairs will be upside down and evil will come. So then what do you need? You need Allāh's words that will guide you, and the words or knowledge of His Prophet ﷺ that will cure you. Allāh ﷻ guides and Prophet cures. Allāh shows you the way; that is His will, and Prophet shows you what you need. *Awlīyāullāh* take from the heart of Prophet ﷺ as he guided the *Ṣaḥābah* ﷺ. *Awlīyāullāh* can follow the way of *Ṣaḥābah* ﷺ, how they interacted with Sayyīdinā Muḥammad ﷺ, the Seal of Messengers.

Wa āhlu 'l-ḥaqq idhā sami'ū al-laghwa 'ariḍū 'anhu. wa idhā sami'ū al-ḥaqq aqbalū 'alayh.
And if People of Truth hear nonsense they leave it, and if they hear words of truth they run to it.

Wa man yaqtarif ḥasanatan nazid lahu fīhā ḥusnā.
And if any one earns any good, We shall give him an increase of good in respect thereof. (Sūrat ash-Shūrā', 42:23)

"And those We reward more and more." So these are some of the characteristics of *awlīyāullāh* and *inshā'Allāh* in this series we will explain more, and describe the levels of different *awlīyā*.

May Allāh ﷻ forgive us and may Allāh ﷻ bless us.

Wa min Allāhi 't-tawfiq, bi ḥurmati 'l-ḥabīb, bi ḥurmati 'l-Fātiḥah.
And with Allāh is success. For the sake of the Beloved, for his sake we recite the opening chapter of Holy Qur'an.

The Story of Imam Ahmad ibn Hanbal

*A'ūdhu billāhi min ash-Shayṭāni 'r-rajīm. Bismillāhi' r-Raḥmāni 'r-Raḥīm.
Nawaytu 'l-arbā'īn, nawaytu 'l-'itikāf, nawaytu'l-khalwah, nawaytu 'l-'uzlah,
nawaytu 'r-riyāḍa, nawaytu 's-sulūk, lillāhi Ta'alā fī hādhā 'l-masjid.
Atī'ūllāha wa atī'ū 'r-Rasūla wa ūli 'l-amri minkum. (4:59)*

If some people don't have eyeglasses they can't see, and with eyeglasses they see. So eyeglasses are important for those who don't have perfect vision, and if they don't have perfect vision, they are nearsighted, measuring minus one, minus two, three, or four, up to minus twenty, which is total blindness. And also a person might be farsighted. If you can't see, you need eyeglasses, which means you need someone to show you the way. And that's why Abū Yazīd al-Bistāmi ق, one of the greatest *awlīyāullāh*, said, *man lam yakun lahu ustādh fa imāmahu 'sh-Shayṭān*, "Who doesn't have a guide, his *imām* is Shayṭān, the devil." And it is said, *man lam yakun lahu shaykh fa-shaykhahu 'sh-Shayṭān*, "Who doesn't have a shaykh, his shaykh is whatever gossips come to his heart, and he will follow that."

So *awlīyāullāh* reach that station not because of their progress in scholarly matters, but because their guides guided them. So the importance is on the guide: how strong he is and how much power he has to guide those who are listening and following his teachings. That is very important to know and understand. It's not so easy that you will be able to reach higher stations by reading books and studying, but it's important to reach when your guide is teaching, and Allāh ﷻ guided everyone to something or someone. He guided the *Ṣaḥābah* ؓ and *Ummat an-Nabī* to Prophet ﷺ, who said, "Whoever you follow from my *Ṣaḥābah*, you will be rightly guided."

This is an example from one of the biggest scholarly shaykhs and many people follow his *madhhab*, that in his time two big *imāms* of Islam were following, like teacher and student: Imām Shafi'ī ق and Imām Aḥmad ibn Ḥanbal ق. Imām Aḥmad ibn Ḥanbal was following Imām Shafi'ī , and after Imām Shafi'ī passed away, Imām Aḥmad ibn Ḥanbal established his own school of thought, which today many people follow. He was a very scholarly person, and all of the *a'immah* (Imāms) were, but this is one example.

One time Imām Aḥmad ibn Ḥanbal was in an association with Imām Shafiʿī and suddenly one *walīyullāh* came, whom Imām Shafiʿī respected a lot. And I heard from Grandshaykh ق, and it is very well established in Sharīʿah that the water from ablution is dead water because it takes all your sins and illnesses. The water of *wuḍū* cleans you and then it becomes dead and you can't use it. That's why some people throw it in the garden or outside, because you can't consume it. So they were discussing some issues and Grandshaykh ق said, "When that *walī* came to Imām Shafiʿī's association, not talking, only listening, people didn't give attention to him. But when he made ablution, Imām Shafiʿī used to drink that water, although he knew in Sharīʿah you can't drink it, but he drank it for *barakah*.

The Lesson from Shayban ar-Rayy

That was Shaybān ar-Rāyy ق, a very high *walī* who was also *ummi*, illiterate, but Allāh ﷻ doesn't look at who is literate or illiterate, and He made his heart and tongue connect.

So Shaybān ar-Rāyy ق came and sat with them in their association and at that moment Imām Aḥmad ibn Ḥanbal looked at Imām Shafiʿī and said, "O my shaykh! *li unnabīh hādha ʿalā nuqsāna ʿilmihi.* I want to emphasize and bring to the attention of that person!" He didn't call Shaybān ar-Rāyy by name, he only said, "that person," not giving importance. "He must complete his knowledge as he doesn't know anything!" Then he pointed to Shaybān ar-Rāyy, saying, "I want to bring to his attention that he is lacking *ʿilm, li yashtaghil li tahsīli hādha 'l-ʿilm,* so he will go and learn a little bit."

Today they say you need a certificate, a paper that says you are an *ʿālim,* or else they consider you are nothing. How do they know you are nothing? Shaybān ar-Rāyy ق didn't know how to read or write, and Imām Aḥmad ibn Ḥanbal ق wasn't giving him importance.

Imām Shafiʿī ق said, "Wait, don't say anything or he will humiliate you!"

Aḥmad ibn Ḥanbal insisted, "No! My duty is to make him aware that he has no knowledge!"

Today if you don't have doctorate, if you are not a PhD, they think you don't know anything; for them, you have to be a doctor of Sharīʿah, but that *walī* is not a doctor in Sharīʿah. That means *awlīyāullāh* don't know that (knowledge from papers), only Allāh ﷻ chooses them. When Allāh chooses them, it is finished.

Wa ʿanā 'khtartuka fastamiʿ limā yūḥā.

I have chosen you; listen then to the inspiration (sent to you). (Ṭāhā, 20:13)

Allāh ﷻ said to Sayyīdinā Mūsā ﷺ, "If you know Sharīʿah or not, I choose you." Allāh chooses His *awlīyā*, and not everyone becomes *walī*. But when Allāh chooses, the matter is finished. Allāh said, *anā 'khtartuka fastamiʿ limā yūḥā*, "Listen to what I am giving you and go and deliver it."

Bismillāhi' r-Raḥmāni 'r-Raḥīm.

Yā ayyuha 'l-muddaththir, qum fa andhir wa rabbaka fakabbir wa thīyābaka faṭāhhir wa 'r-rujza fahjur.

O you wrapped in your cloak! Arise and warn! Your Lord magnify, your garment purify, and pollution shun. (Sūrat al-Muddaththir, 74:1-5)

"O Muḥammad! You, the one who is covering yourself." Prophet ﷺ was shivering at that time, *qum fa andhur*, "Wake up, go and deliver the message, and glorify your Lord." *Wa thīyābaka faṭahhir*, "And go purify your clothes." Which clothes; what we wear, or the clothes of the heart? They cover this physical body, which is the cover of the heart, a piece of flesh, but what is inside it? Can Allāh not put inside the flesh what He put inside *Kaʿbah*? What is inside *Kaʿbah*? It is four walls and inside are *asrārullāh*, Allāh's secrets, and what He manifested on that House no one knows, just as what He put in the heart of Prophet no one knows!

Fa-kayfa idhā ji'nā min kulli ummatin bi-shahīdin wa ji'nā bika ʿalā hā ūlā'i shahīdā.

How then if We brought from each people a witness, and We brought you as a witness against these people! (Sūrat an-Nisa, 4:41)

"When we have brought from every *ummah* a *shahīd*, witness." That means Allāh chose a witness from every *ummah*. *Wa ji'na bika ʿalā hāūlā'i shahīda*, "And We have brought you, O Muḥammad, as a witness over all of them." That means, "We brought these prophets first and then *awlīyāullāh* as witnesses on their followers that are on the right path and rightly guided, and We are not confirming that until you, *yā* Muḥammad, make witness on all of them, the prophets and the *awlīyā*!"

Was Sayyīdinā Mūsā ﷺ educated? No. It means if Allāh ﷻ chooses, He chooses. And Sayyīdinā Muḥammad ﷺ is *nabī al-ummī,* the prophet who never opened a book or read. Today, what is knowledge? Show me what do they teach in Azhar ash-Sharīf, in Shām, Morocco, or Hijāz? They teach what is in books and no longer give importance to spiritual knowledge. Let the shaykhs of Azhar go to where Imām Shafiʿī ق is buried there.

This story is from two main scholars, Imām Shafiʿī and Imām Aḥmad ibn Ḥanbal. Imām Shafiʿī was following Shaybān ar-Rāyy and said to Imām Aḥmad, *lā takūn jassūran,* "Don't encourage yourself to question him as he will humiliate you.

He said, "No, no, no! My job is to tell him he needs this kind of teaching and to go and learn.

And Imām Shafiʿī said, *lā tafʿal,* "Don't touch on that subject; leave him alone."

And Imām Aḥmad asked Shaybān ar-Rāyy, *madhā taqūl fiman nasīya ṣalātuh min aṣ-ṣalawāt al-khams fi 'l-Islām, fi 'sh-sharīʿah,* "What is the judgment of someone that the time of the prayer passed and he didn't pray, he forgot?" It needs knowledge. Today there are too many different schools of thought and they give different answers. Like the Wahhabis and Salafis say, "Don't repeat it as the time is gone, so even if you pray *qadā,* make it up, it is not accepted."

They believe there is no *qadā,* but other schools of thought say it is an obligation to make it up, and they believe that *qadā* prayer it is not perfect, but nevertheless you have to make it up so you will learn discipline. Those are two different schools.

So Imām Aḥmad was checking Shaybān ar-Rāyy and said, "You don't know anything! What is the *ḥukum*? Give me the judgment of Sharīʿah. What do we say to this question? Give me a *fatwa.*" Shaybān ar-Rāyy laughed and Imām Aḥmad became more frustrated, he wanted to humiliate him in front of Imām Shafiʿī .

Shaybān ar-Rāyy answered, "*Yā* Aḥmad! Are you challenging me?"

Aḥmad ibn Ḥanbal began to shake, and Shaybān ar-Rāyy said, "Your question is like that of a child. How dare you ask me such a question? Don't you know you are ignorant for asking that? *Yā* Aḥmad, *qalbun ghafala ʿan Allāh fa yanbaghī an yu'addab ḥattā la yaʿūd ilā ghaflatihi,* a heart that becomes heedless of Allāh's Presence for one moment must be disciplined. That means you must be disciplined when you come and ask such a question. How dare you ask someone whose heart is with his Lord in every moment, that if he misses a prayer what he has to do! If you miss a prayer you have to be disciplined, *ḥattā la ya'ūd ilā ghaflatihi.* That means, don't ask that childish question! Your heart has to be in Allāh's Presence, if your heart is there you will never miss a prayer."

That is like someone who has no heart, what will happen? Throw him in the grave. That heart must be disciplined so you don't become heedless another time. And at that moment Imām Aḥmad fainted, he had a heart attack from the power of those words of Shaybān ar-Rāyy.

Imām Shafi'ī said, "Leave him until he comes back to normal and leaves asking such childish questions." When he woke up, Imām Shafi'ī said to him, *alam aqul laka lam tata'arad lahu,* "Didn't I tell you not to bother him? So don't bother him! If you bother him, this is your end."

Don't bother *awlīyāullāh*; don't come against them or they will make you to faint. What happened to Sayyīdinā Mūsā ﷺ? He fainted! He said, "O my Lord, let me see You." You cannot; when Allāh ﷻ wills, you will see without questioning. Allāh made him faint to make him learn. That is why *awlīyāullāh* are always fainting in Allāh's Divine Presence, surrendering. So don't come to a *walī* and criticize; they will humiliate you from their powers.

And I heard the continuation of this story from Grandshaykh ق: When Imām Aḥmad woke up he crawled on his chest to Shaybān ar-Rāyy, asking for forgiveness and seeking his guidance.

So two *imāms* were taking from Shaybān ar-Rāyy and he was illiterate! Also, Imām Abū Hanīfa bin Nu'man ق took knowledge from Bishr al-Hāfi ق. If an *ummī*, one who cannot read or write, is a powerful *walī* that is able to put down Imām Aḥmad ibn Ḥanbal, what do you think about a *walī* who is literate, who knows everything? What about his power; what can he do? If you see that one *ummī* from *awlīyā* has this power, what do you think if Allāh gives them heavenly knowledge, then what can they do? They can make a hole in the boat!

> *Fantalaqa ḥattā idha rakiba fi as-safinati kharaqaha. Qāla akharaqtaha li tughriqa ahlaha. Laqad ji'ta shay'ān 'imrā.*
> *So the two set out until, when they were in the ship, he made a hole in it. (Moses) said, "Have you made a hole to drown the folk therein? Verily you have done a dreadful thing!"* (Sūrat al-Kahf, 18:71)

What did Sayyīdinā Khiḍr ﷺ do? He made a hole in the boat, then killed the boy, and then he built the wall. So he drowns you to take all your bad characteristics, and then he kills your ego, and then he builds the wall of treasures in your heart. So don't bother *awlīyāullāh,* because they have many ways to bother you. In every moment of your life they can bother you!

Grandshaykh ق said, "Every day the shaykh has to look at the *murīd* three times. When he looks he doesn't send candies, but he sends him poison, to check if they are handling difficulty or not." So when you get in difficulty remember that your shaykh is looking at you, and don't get angry. I am not speaking about business difficulties, I am talking about *murīd*-to-*murīd,* or people-to-people, who get angry with each other, who lie about what they are doing, and this and that. Be careful and remember at that moment the shaykh is observing you. That is why today, I am going to tell these two *(murīds)* not to go back home, but to stay here! (laughter)

So that is why they said, *laylī bi wajhika mushriqun wa ẓalāmahu fi 'n-nāsi sāri,* "My night in your face is daylight," or, "When I am looking at your face, O my shaykh, my night is daylight shining. Even if it is night, when I look at your face in dark nights I see that *ḍīyā,* that shining of the sun on Earth. Your face is shining, *wa ẓalāmahu fi 'n-nāsi sāri,* but the darkness of the night in the faces of the people is dark, but in your face it is sunlight. *Wa 'n-nāsu fī sadaf aẓ-ẓalāmi,* and the people are in darkness, *wa lākin naḥnu fī ḍaw an-nahār,* and we are with you, O our shaykh, O our *walī,* in the daylight." That means, "When you are among us it is daylight, but when we are with people it is darkness." That is why we always have to watch what we are doing, what we are saying, and what we are putting in our hearts.

It is said that Rābiʿah al-ʿAdawiyyah ق got sick. They asked her, "What is the cause of your illness? Why are you sick?" She didn't have the flu, a heart attack, or any physical sickness, but spiritually she was depressed. They asked her, "Why are you depressed?"

Today if you ask people, "What are you doing?" they will answer, "I am getting counseling from a psychologist." He is a psychologist who himself needs a psychiatrist! If you need a psychologist, go to a *walī* because he knows your needs.

Rābiʿah al-ʿAdawiyyah ق said, "Oh, I have a major problem."

They said, "You, a lady saint?"

And ladies complain they have no saints! There are many. The Prophet's wives are *Ummuhāt al-Mu'minīn,* "Mothers of All Believers" ﷺ.

No one can reach their ranks, or the ranks of the lady Companions of Prophet ﷺ or the lady teachers after them. But this psychological problem is in the minds of ladies because of the rudeness of men.

They said, "Why are you depressed? Did anyone from the *jama'at* bother you?"

She said, *wa lākin naẓartu ilā 'l-jannata bi 'l-qalb,* "No. I gazed at the Heavens with my heart. I was in a trance, a spiritual state, and that opened, and I looked at the Heavens through my heart."

To us that is good, but for her it was not good, because she made a mistake according to her rank. *Fa ghāra 'alayya qalbī,* "My heart got jealous from me, because my heart doesn't want to have partners or have anyone other than Allāh ﷻ. It asked, how am I looking through my heart to Paradise when I have to look with my heart to Allāh ﷻ? I fell into this big sin, this mistake."

Look how they are so sensitive when their heart moves a little bit! Although she was looking at the Heavens, she moved one second to heedlessness. For us it is perfect, but for her it was a heedless moment that her heart went to look at Paradise and left looking at Allāh ﷻ.

Her heart asked, "How do you dare look at Paradise? I (your heart) has to always be in that Divine Presence!" That's why Prophet ﷺ said:

Lī wajhun ma' Allāh wa lī wajhun ma' al-khalq.
I have one face (presence) with Allāh, and I have one face with the ummah.

That means, "I don't let anything interfere," *yaghār 'alā awlīyā'ihi wa anbīyā'ihi.* Allāh ﷻ doesn't like to share anyone with His servants! We will continue tomorrow about *Ḥaqīqat al-Ghīrah*, the Reality of Jealousy, and what is the jealousy that *awlīyāullāh* are trying to get rid of. So it means, be aware of the power of your shaykh. Don't let anyone share with you your love to your shaykh. Your love must be to your shaykh, from your shaykh to Prophet ﷺ, and from Prophet to Allāh ﷻ.

So Shaybān ar-Rāyy ق scolded Imām Aḥmad ق, saying, "Why are you asking me about missing prayers when every moment I am in prayer? How can you miss a prayer when you are always in that Presence? That prayer time is heavenly time." Shaybān ar-Rāyy is showing him, "Not only am I praying in *dunyā* time, but in heavenly time also. Do you know heavenly time, O Aḥmad?"

"No, I only know *dunyā* time."

One time Grandshaykh ق and Mawlana Shaykh ق said that Sayyīdinā
Bilāl ؓ was standing to call *adhān*, and Prophet ﷺ said, "Wait," and as soon
as he said, "Don't call *adhān*," he said, "Call *adhān*." Sayyīdinā Bilāl was
surprised. Prophet explained, "The moment from when I said 'wait' to the
time I said 'call', the sun moved fifty thousand years." That means in that
moment the *Bayt al-Mā'mūr* moved. The reality of *Ka'bah* is the reflection of
Bayt al-Mā'mūr, the real House of Allāh ﷻ located in the Fourth Heaven,
where Prophet ﷺ prayed with all prophets in *Laylat al-'Isrā' wal-Mi'rāj*.

So *adhān* is not on our time, it is on the time that Prophet accepted in
the holy night; he established the times and we pray on the time of *Bayt al-
Mā'mūr* in Mecca and Madinah. It is not when we pray *Zhuhr* in America,
for (by then) already it was prayed in the Heavens! But the right time was
what Prophet ﷺ established. Allāh ﷻ (accepts our prayer) as made at the
right time, but in reality, the right time is when Prophet prays.

Who can give you such knowledge if not an inheritor of the secrets of
Prophet? You don't know how *awlīyāullāh* act and what they know, from
knowledge they inherited from the heart of Sayyīdinā Muḥammad ﷺ! That
is why we must not object on how they do things; what they do is according
to the Prophet ﷺ, who did not pray except on the right time.

According to a *ḥadīth* in Bukhari and Muslim, it was near the time of
Maghrib, and Prophet asked Sayyīdinā 'Alī ؓ, "Did you pray *'Aṣr*?"
He said, "Yā Rasūlullāh, I did not." So Prophet ﷺ stopped the sun for
Sayyīdinā 'Alī ؓ until he finished praying, and then it went to sunset. So
Prophet's power is but a drop and he gives drops to *awlīyāullāh*. All of them
have one drop from that ocean of Prophet's knowledge, and that keep
things moving until the Day of Judgment.

May Allāh bless us, forgive us, and grant our shaykh long life, and
make all of us happy, healthy and wealthy!

Wa min Allāhi 't-tawfīq, bi ḥurmati 'l-ḥabīb, bi ḥurmati 'l-Fātiḥah.
*And with Allāh is success. For the sake of the Beloved, for his sake we recite
the opening chapter of Holy Qur'an.*

Allah's Possessiveness

A'ūdhu billāhi min ash-Shayṭāni 'r-rajīm. Bismillāhi' r-Raḥmāni 'r-Raḥīm. Nawaytu 'l-arbā'īn, nawaytu 'l-'itikāf, nawaytu'l-khalwah, nawaytu 'l-'uzlah, nawaytu 'r-riyāḍa, nawaytu 's-sulūk, lillāhi Ta'alā fi hādhā 'l-masjid. Atī'ūllāha wa atī'ū 'r-Rasūla wa ūli 'l-amri minkum. (4:59)

Who does not have a shaykh, his shaykh is Shayṭān; he comes at the right time to deviate us from the real path. People ask, "Why are we speaking of Shayṭān and devils? We are praying, fasting, doing this and that." It is true, we are praying and fasting in our eyes, but in Allāh's eyes, Shayṭān is still playing with us, as he played with Adam ﷺ in Heavens. Isn't Shayṭān able to play with us on Earth then? He can. That is why you always need a guard.

Today if you travel to Malaysia or Indonesia, you see a hired guard at the entry to every house. Why? Although Malaysia is a country with not too much crime, but still they are hiring guards because they don't want to fall into a heedless moment and suddenly something happens, so they are taking care. Likewise, we have to take care by understanding and knowing that at any moment we might fall into heedlessness and if we don't have a shaykh to guide us, we fall into the miseries of this *dunyā*. Allāh ﷻ sent messengers. He has messengers and He has prophets. A prophet is not a messenger, although a messenger is a prophet and a messenger at the same time, *Saḥib ar-Risalah*.

Wa mā arsalnā min rasūlin illa li yutā'a bi idhnillāhi wa law annahum idh ẓalamū anfusahum jā'ūka fastaghfarullāh wa 'staghfara lahumu 'r-rasūla la-wajadūllāha tawwāban raḥīmā.
We sent an apostle, but to be obeyed in accordance with the Will of Allāh. If they had only when they were unjust to themselves come to you and asked Allāh's forgiveness, and the Messenger had asked forgiveness for them, they would have found Allāh indeed Oft-Returning, Most Merciful.

(Sūrat an-Nisa, 4:64)

The messenger has a message to deliver so you have to obey his message, while a prophet does not have a message to deliver; he obeys the messenger of his time or the messenger that came before him. So any prophet who is not a messenger must obey the messenger that came before or the messenger who is in his time.

Allāh has appointed many prophets. What is the *hikmat* (wisdom) of appointing many prophets if they don't have a message? Why did they become prophets? We understand that a messenger has a constitution and Sharīʿah, and Allāh sent him with that message to follow it. But a prophet can be in the same time of a messenger. So who follows whom? A prophet follows a messenger, a messenger doesn't follow a prophet. So every messenger that came, was a cycle of this lifetime. Allāh sent messengers and ended them with the seal of Messengers, Sayyīdinā Muḥammad ﷺ. That is why Islam orders us to accept all the messengers that came before the Prophet.

Wa mā arsalnā min rasūlin illa an yutāʿa bi idhnillāhi. He didn't say, "we didn't send a *nabī*," He said, "we didn't send a messenger until he will be obeyed." So Prophet wrapped all messengers that came before. But it is not necessary to accept prophets that came before as you have Sayyīdinā Muḥammad ﷺ as a messenger. But prophets are appointed to accept the messenger that came before them and in their time. Why? Because we have must have a role model. If there is a messenger in the east, there was no technology at that time, it was not opened yet, it opened in the time of Prophet. There was no tech to reach (far) and so Allāh sent messengers and prophets; "prophets" means *ʿibādAllāh aṣ-ṣāliḥīn*, servants that are symbols, role models for everyone.

Prophet ﷺ mentioned "*Maqām al-Iḥsān*," to worship Allāh as if you are seeing Him. And if you are not seeing Him, know that He is seeing you. So Allāh sent prophets as role models to be symbols for the community around them.

> *Yā ayyuhalladhīna āmanū ittaqūllāh wa kūnū maʿ aṣ-ṣādiqīn.*
> *O you who believe! Fear Allāh and be those who are pious (in word and deed).* (Sūrat at-Tawbah, 9:119)

So that is an indicator to be with prophets in the time before the Prophet. They are trustworthy ones, and thus are symbols and examples for their communities in their time, as *awlīyāullāh* are today. There are no more prophets or messengers after Sayyīdinā Muḥammad ﷺ. There are inheritors of the pious and sincere people, the prophets, and they are *awlīyāullāh*. Some *awlīyāullāh* carry knowledge they take from the heart of the Prophet and that is how they guide their followers. Some take with a prophet who had no message but who was pious. So they dress in that piety and become a role model between their communities.

This is a very, very important point in our understanding and the teaching. That is why Allāh ﷻ said, as mentioned by Prophet ﷺ:

> *Min al-mu'minīna rijālun ṣadaqū mā ʿaḥadullāha ʿalayh. Fa minhum man qaḍā naḥbahu wa minhum man yantaẓir wa mā badalū tabdīla.*
> *Among the believers are Men who accepted and did what they promised of the Covenant they took with Allāh. Of them some have completed their vow (to the extreme), and some (still) wait, but they have never changed (their determination) in the least.* (Sūrat al-'Aḥzāb, 33:23)

They are men who kept their covenant and did their best in *dunyā*. Some of them left and some are living. They are passing away slowly with time and others are coming in their turn. They are the real models whom we can learn from. Not every *murīd* is a *walī* or a role model. The shaykh picks up or appoints some role models because he wants the *barakah* to be spread. These people might not have knowledge to guide, but the shaykh appoints them as they are sincere and pious to do *dhikrūllāh*, as when Prophet ﷺ was asked by one *Ṣaḥābī*:

> *Yā Rasūlullāh, inna sharīʿah al-islām qad kathurat ʿalayya, "The rules of Islām became heavy on me." Prophet ﷺ said, lā yazāl lisānak raṭban bi-dhikrillāh, "Make your tongue wet (alive) with dhikrūllāh."*(Tirmidhī)

So those who make themselves busy with *dhikrūllāh* are pious ones. They are not necessarily *murshidīn* to guide you through knowledge, but they are like blending a beautiful smell, as when someone with a nice scent comes in and makes everyone smell that way. It is like a rose that makes everyone in its environment smell nice. One of these *awlīyāullāh* is appointed by the shaykh.

That is why Sayyīdinā Abū Yazīd al-Bistāmi ق said, "Who has no shaykh, Shayṭān is his shaykh." Why? Because Shayṭān will bring him stinky roses and will guide him not to remember *dhikrūllāh*. The one who does *dhikr* will have a nice smell. The Prophet ﷺ said, "The smell of a fasting person's mouth is better than the smell of Paradise." Because the angels approach the fasting person and reflect their smell on them. So the person disobeying Allāh will smell of Shayṭān, bad smell. This is *ʿilmu 's-sulūk*, knowledge of that journey where you are going, to Allāh's Divine Presence. *As-sālik* is the one who is following the path.

Each one of us has a different way or journey. Our journey is full of miseries because we are blending it with *dunyā* work. But *awlīyā's* journey is perfect. If you follow that *walī* or that role model, you will reach your destiny and he will bring you to the Divine Presence. That is why a guide is important in the lives of people. As we said, there are two types of guides; the one spreading the teaching of Prophet ﷺ and Islam, and the one who is a role model, who guides through his behavior. He has *Maqām al-Iḥsān*, the Station of Perfected Character. You like his ways and you follow him. He doesn't need to say anything to you. That is why you have many different kinds *awlīyāullāh*. They are, Budalā, Nujabā, Nuqabā, Awtād, and Akhyār. They are everywhere to guide the *ummah* through their destinies. So Allāh ﷻ has chosen, as He chose His prophets and His messengers, from *Ummat an-Nabī* ﷺ guides that carry and inherit knowledges continuously from the heart of Prophet and spread it.

Some are only to be role models for others and Allāh loves them. He doesn't like their love to be for other than Him; it has to be to Him only. That is why in *ṭarīqah* there is *gharīh*, not in the meaning of jealousy, but *karāhat mushārakat li-ghayrih* (hatred of sharing with anyone else), but possessiveness. You dislike that someone shares the love of your beloved. If you love someone, you want that one to be to yours only, and it is not jealousy. You feel, "I don't like anyone to share that love except me."

Let us give an example. A husband doesn't like to share anyone with his wife and a wife doesn't like to share anyone with her husband; that is *ghīrah*. So in another meaning, Allāh chose his saints and He doesn't like His saints to share their love with anyone, it must be exclusively to Him.

The students of the shaykh have to know that the final level of their love is to reach the Divine Presence and love to Allāh ﷻ! That is why we say *maḥabbat ash-shaykh* guides you to *maḥabbat an-Nabī* ﷺ, which guides you to *maḥabbat Allāh*, which is the last landing. This means that you don't see anyone in your life. In every *ʿamal*, action, you do or every moment of life passes, you have to see the Will of Allāh ﷻ, no one else. If you don't do that as a *walī,* Allāh doesn't like it. He likes His *walī* only to be to Him. That is why He likes the heart of His servant not to be attached to anyone.

The Genuine Taste of Divine Love

When Rābiʿah al-ʿAdawiyyah ق got sick, they asked her, what is the problem? She said, "I looked at Paradise with my heart. That was a mistake. I looked with my heart at something created and my heart must be only for my Lord." *Maqām al-Wilayat* it is not easy to reach. That is why these *awlīyā, Aqṭāb, Budalā, Nuqabā, Nujabā, Awtād,* and *Akhyār,* have excellent characteristics. We are only able to speak about it, but they are able to taste it. We are not tasting, we are only listening and reading, but they are listening and tasting. Adam ﷺ listened to Iblīs and he lost. That is why Prophet ﷺ said:

> *Ḥubbuka li shay yaʿmī wa yaṣum.*
> *O my Lord! Your Love to someone will make that one blind and deaf.*

Your love to someone or to any of your Creation, will make that one blind and deaf. It means Allāh has *ghīrah;* He doesn't like anyone to share His servant and wants the love of that servant directed only to Him. And when He loves that servant completely, that servant becomes blind and deaf to this *dunyā;* he cannot see and hear anything of this world, he only hears and sees Allāh ﷻ. That is why Prophet ﷺ said:

> *Lī saʿatun maʿ al-khāliq wa lī saʿatun maʿ al-khalq.*
> *I have a picture or an hour with My Lord in which no angels can be in the middle of that relationship.*

Prophet Muḥammad's ﷺ heart is completely blind from *dunyā,* although he is not, but in the meaning and he is deaf and blind from *dunyā.* That is why he was invited to *Miʿrāj,* where no angel reached. At the Station of *Qāba Qawsayni aw Adnā,* he is not seeing or feeling anything but the Divine Presence of His Lord. Grandshaykh ق said Allāh asked him there, "Who are you?" and Prophet said, "I am You."

That is the real *tawḥīd* for the Prophet! He understood the level of Oneness, that in the Divine Presence everything was not existing, and *awlīyāullāh* quench their thirst from that ocean. When you are near, you are not seeing anything except Holy Divine Attributes that Allāh will be manifesting on you. *Wa al-ḥaqqu anna al-ghīratu lillāh ḥaqqan,* "The reality is, Allāh has the right not to share anything of His servants with Him."

Allāh ﷻ said:

Awliyāī taḥta qibābī la ya'lamahum ghayrī.
My awlīyā are under My domes; no one knows them except Me.
(*Ḥadīth Qudsī*)

Man 'adā lī walīyyan faqad ādhantahu bi 'l-ḥarb.
Whoever comes against a walī (friend) of Mine, I declare war on him.
(*Ḥadīth Qudsī*)

That is *ghīrah.* So Allāh's servants have no right; all their actions, all their breaths, and all their remembrance must be only for Allāh ﷻ. When someone has *ghīrah,* it means he loves someone and doesn't want to share. This shows there is love there. *Ghīrah* takes you to love. When you become pious, *ghīrah* to Allāh comes to you and when that happens, *maḥabbatAllāh* blows to you. So then you enter the first level of *maḥabbatAllāh, maḥabbat al-habīb, and maḥabbat al-shaykh,* which leads to *hudūr,* and then that leads to annihilation.

It is said, *al-ghīra ghīratān,* possessiveness, jealousy, is of two kinds: *ghīrat al-bashar 'alā an-nufūs wa ghīratallāh 'alā al-qulūb,* the possessiveness of the self, the body loves the ego and the ego leads to bad desires. When body is attached to the ego, then you are making a detour and that is why we call it *al-ghīrat al-bashariyya 'alā an-nufūs.* The body doesn't want to share anything with the self. The ego must be "for the body only" and that is where Shayṭān can play.

But there is the second part; *ghīratallāh 'alā al-qulūb,* the heavenly *ghīrah* which is on the hearts, as it is said, *ma fi qalbī illa-Llāh,* "There is nothing in my heart except Allāh." So the heart is the House of Allāh ﷻ. Constantly for twenty-four hours that heart is in *dhikrūllāh.* If you put a speaker on the heart, you can hear it saying, *Hū, Hū, Hū.* You see these palpitations in this sound. That is a sound that has been coded and covered.

Everyone has a code in their heart; if they open it, they will understand what kind of *dhikr* their heart is doing. And every person's *dhikr* doesn't resemble the *dhikr* of another. Even if both say *Hū,* each one will be different from the other or else, that will diminish Allāh's Greatness. Just as every angel has a different *dhikr,* each person's heart has a *dhikr,* voluntary or involuntary. The human being is born on *fitrah*, on the natural way, but his parents make him either Christian, Jewish, or Zoroastrian. But you are born on *fitratu 'l-Islām*, and that is the light put in the heart of people.

Inna ad-dīna 'ind-Allāhi al-Islām.
The religion before Allāh is Islām. (Sūrat 'Āli 'Imrān, 3:19)

All religion ends up in Islam, even from Adam 🕊 and Ibrāhīm 🕊, who said:

Innī wajahut wajhiyya lil-ladhī fatar as-samāwāti wal-'arḍa hanīfa musliman.
I have directed my face to The One Who created Heaven and Earth and I am Muslim.

It is from that time. So the religion to Allāh is Islam as it came last, but it came with Ibrāhīm 🕊 and ended with Prophet 🕊 wrapping everything together. The hearts of human beings are created and born on Islam, that is why it is voluntary or involuntary, and that is why it is making that *dhikr* by pumping. When the heart stops pumping, you are finished. If the brain stops you are still alive, but if the heart stops you are dead. Allāh doesn't like His servant's heart doing anything other than remembering Him. When Allāh loves someone, He wants that one to be for Him only.

One of the *awlīyā* said, "Why did Allāh send Adam on Earth?"

Al-Qushayrī ق said, "The example of this is Adam whose homeland was Paradise living there eternally, with all its delicious tastes, then Allāh became possessive of him. Adam loved to be live for eternity in Paradise, which Allāh did not accept. To show him that Allāh does not accept his self to love other than Him. Allāh does not become harmed by someone but you will be harmed by losing Allāh.

And he said, "When Ibrāhīm became so fond of Ismā'īl, Allāh said to go slaughter him," as there can be no competition, no love for anyone else in the hearts of His servants. Prophets have no love except to their Creator, and here we are speaking of real love. When Ismā'īl was born, Ibrāhīm was so happy that his love went to Ismā'īl. That is why today humans are receiving that kind of love for their children, which is okay. But for Ibrāhīm, Allāh said, "Go and slaughter your son, Ismā'īl."

So Allāh told Ibrāhīm to slaughter Ismā'īl, and when Ibrāhīm took the knife to slaughter Ismā'īl, at that moment Allāh 🕊 took his love for 'Ismā'īl out of his heart, then He sent the lamb to be slaughtered. But Adam 🕊

wanted to be eternally in Paradise. So for Ibrāhīm ☼, Allāh accepted his intention to slaughter, saying, "That is enough for Me."

Dhikrūllāh is important. That is why the guidance of *shuyūkh* took their followers to *dhikrūllāh*. Mawlana Shaykh Nazim ق says that even if two people have homes next to each other, both do *dhikr* to increase the *tajallī*."

May Allāh give long life to Mawlana Shaykh Nazim ق! May Allāh ﷻ forgive us and may Allāh ﷻ bless us.

Wa min Allāhi 't-tawfīq, bi ḥurmati 'l-ḥabīb, bi ḥurmati 'l-Fātiḥah.
And with Allāh is success. For the sake of the Beloved, for his sake we recite the opening chapter of Holy Qur'an.

Ittiba and Taqleed: Follow the Footsteps and Imitate the Pious

A'ūdhu billāhi min ash-Shayṭāni 'r-rajīm. Bismillāhi' r-Raḥmāni 'r-Raḥīm.
Nawaytu 'l-arbā'īn, nawaytu 'l-'itikāf, nawaytu'l-khalwah, nawaytu 'l-'uzlah,
nawaytu 'r-riyāḍa, nawaytu 's-sulūk, lillāhi Ta'alā fī hādhā 'l-masjid.
Atī'ūllāha wa atī'ū 'r-Rasūla wa ūli 'l-amri minkum. (4:59)

Awlīyāullāh, qaddas-Allāhu Ta'alā arwāḥahumu zakīyya wa nawwar-Allāhu Ta'alā aḍriḥatahum al-mubāraka, may Allāh ﷻ bless their souls, those who passed away and those living. Awlīyāullāh always cared for their followers. As we said yesterday, if Allāh likes His servant He is possessive of that one; He doesn't want His servant to go anywhere. That is why the end-goal of a servant is to be in the Divine Presence and the shaykhs have to do their best for their followers to reach there, as this is their duty. And awlīyā were not able to become awlīyā except by inkisār, to lower themselves to be like Earth for their followers.

If you step on the Earth, it doesn't complain; if you drill it, take its treasures, mine it, or throw garbage on it, it doesn't complain. A walī is like the Earth; he doesn't complain. He wants those whom he is guiding to benefit and they didn't reach that level except through humiliation and humility.

Humility means to show they are like normal people. I am speaking of the Naqshbandi Ṭarīqah and other ṭarīqahs. In the Naqshbandi Ṭarīqah, the shaykh doesn't show himself with any abnormality, he always shows himself as normal, in order to make familiarity with followers. They even joke with their followers, as they are following the footsteps of the Prophet.

He used to sit privately with Ṣaḥābah ☺ and joke and eat with them to make them feel easy-going. It is not like visiting a government minister, when you have to follow many protocols, although the minister might stand at the door of the Prime Minister like nothing. A Prime Minister might even kick the minister, and we might shake in front of the minister. Even to his doorman we say, "Yes sir." Do we say it (among ourselves)? Never.

Awlīyāullāh don't have that behavior or characteristic because they want to show they are easy-going with followers and that is how their followers are attracted to them, but murīds have to show discipline to their shaykh by keeping the *adab* of following. That is why people say, *hal atabiʿuka.*

Mūsā ﷺ, who is *ūlū 'l-ʿāzam,* one of the Five Highest Prophets, said, "Can I follow?" *Ittibaʿ* means to follow, or "footsteps". That is why *ʿulamā* said you must have *ittibaʿ*, not like today as the Salafi *ʿulamā* say, *lā tatatabiʿ*, "Don't follow, do what you like." No, you have to follow! Sayyīdinā Mūsā ﷺ asked permission from Sayyīdinā Khiḍr ﷺ, "Can I follow you?"

Khiḍr said, "I don't know, you might not be able."

But Mūsā asked; he came with discipline and knocked on the door.

So *ʿulamā* must understand, as *Āhlu 's-Sunnah wa 'l-Jamaʿah,* we have to follow the pious ones who came before us, and imitate them, *taqlīd*. Today they refuse *ittibaʿ* and *taqlīd,* and Allāh ﷻ said He chose messengers and put them among the community for people to follow their footsteps. People look at them and say, "That is a pious one. I have to imitate his way." So that is *ṭarīqah*: to make *taqlīd* and *ittibaʿ*, which is the order in the Holy Qur'an.

So Sayyīdinā Khiḍr said, "If you want to follow me I accept, but you have to be patient." You have to follow a shaykh, yes; you took his hand, you gave initiation, then what is your duty? To follow. One simple example is when Sayyīdinā ʿUbaydullāh al-Ahrār ق said to his *murīd,* "Go to the mountain and wait, I am coming." What did he do? He went to the mountain and he stayed all day; *Maghrib* came and shaykh didn't come. But he was a clever *murīd* and his heart is connected. He said to himself, "O! Shaykh said, 'I am coming.' Why do I have to listen to the ego and go home?" So he stayed and waited and the second day he waited and shaykh didn't come, one week, one month, no more food, the fruit on the trees finished. He didn't say, "I have to go home to sleep," he waited. One year passed, and no shaykh. Then Allāh ﷻ sent a deer to him, because he kept the word of the shaykh, who said, "I am coming, wait for me." That is *ittibaʿ*, to follow.

Sayyīdinā Khiḍr ﷺ said to Sayyīdinā Mūsā ﷺ, "You may follow, but don't object against me."

Qāla innaka lan tastatiʿ maʿiya sabra.
(The other) said, "Verily you will not be able to have patience with me!"
(Sūrat al-Kahf, 18:67)

Don't object. When you object it means there is no *ittibaʿ*. The first step in *ṭarīqah* is *ittibaʿ* and *taqlīd,* and unfortunately today *ʿulamā* are saying, "Don't follow." The principle of *Āhlu 's-Sunnah wa 'l-Jamaʿah* is to follow and take the consensus of the *'ulamā*! That *murīd* waited seven years until his shaykh came, saying, "O my son! Where were you? I might have died and you didn't come to see?"

The *murīd* answered, "If I left, then you would not be here now by order of Prophet." He reached a high level.

What happened yesterday? I said I am coming at 12 o'clock and you ran away, you didn't wait even half-an-hour! This one (*murīd*) ran away. What kind of notes are you taking? Whoever doesn't follow Allāh's orders first, then Prophet's ways and orders and *awliyāullāh's* order and ways, *fa laysa fi yadihi shay*, then he will not achieve anything.

Sayyīdinā 'Alī ☙ said, "The reality is within three things:

Al-haqīqatu fi thalāth: Man lam yakun 'indahu sunnatullāh wa sunnat rasūlihi wa sunnat awliyāihi fa laysa fi yadihi shay.
If someone doesn't have respect for Allāh's way, the Prophet's way and awliyā's way, he or she can't achieve anything.

Prophet ☙ said:
'Ana madinatu 'l-'ilmi wa 'Aliyyun babuha.
I am the city of knowledge and 'Alī is its door.   (al-Ḥākim, Tirmidhī)

His Companions ☙ said, "Tell us what we have to do."

He said, "Allāh's Way is *kitmān as-sirr*, keep the secrets." Don't expose them, keep hiding secrets. That has two meanings here: it means keep whatever Allāh gives you in the way of your journey, don't expose it, or you will feel arrogant and you lose. Don't say, "I am speaking with *jinn*, I will send *jinn* on you, or I will do this and I will do that. " No, show humbleness in every situation (as if) you know nothing; that way you will not show yourself as arrogant. And *kitmān as-sirr*, don't expose your brothers' and sisters' mistakes. Both of these ways are exposing.

If you get secret of what Allāh opened to your heart, you go and say it, especially if they saw a dream. What do they do? They are so happy to tell about their dream. If Allāh wants to show that dream to everyone He can, but He sent it to you. If you want to say it, say it to your shaykh directly, not to people. They come and say to each what they have seen in dreams and expose it on the Internet even, saying, "I have seen a dream." If it is nice a one, keep it for yourself, and secondly, don't expose to your brothers and sisters what Allāh ☙ gave you. What do we do? We expose them! So what we said about, *anā madinatu 'l-'ilmi wa 'Alīyyun bābuhā*, and what *ṭarīqahs* came from Sayyīdinā 'Alī ؎? Don't expose secrets that Allāh has given to you, keep it to yourself. If you did good for humanity, keep it to yourself. If you gave of what Allāh gave you, don't say to people, "I gave." Don't say it, keep it to yourself.

And they asked, "What about the *sunnah* of Prophet, *wa mā hīya sunnat ar-rasūl*?" And this is what *'ulamā* have to know the importance of, and all politicians have to go back to Muslim sources, and extract from pious people what they said, and not to listen to those who are extreme in their understanding.

To Care for All Humanity

They asked Sayyīdinā 'Alī ؎, "What is Prophet's way? We understand Allāh's way to veil what happened to you, but what is the way of Prophet?"

Sayyīdinā 'Alī said, *al-muḍārātu li 'n-nās*. That is very important. O politicians! That is what Islam is based on! He took from the *sunnah* of Prophet ؎ and he didn't say, "Explode yourself with suicide bombings," as we see Muslims killing Muslims now. He said, *al-muḍārātu li 'n-nās*, to be able to take everything balanced, to be caring for everyone, how to deal with him to keep whoever you meet happy. And he said, *li 'n-nās*, "to humanity," not *li 'l-Muslim*, "Muslims (only)." Prophet's way is to make everyone feel they have been cared for. Prophet took everyone into consideration, and this is not easy, but this is what we have to tell people Islam is based on, to take consideration for everyone's needs. Prophet ؎ gave everyone what he or she needed, but who doesn't have a mind or a heart doesn't understand.

They asked, *Qīla wa mā sunnata awlīyā-ih*, "What is the *sunnah* of the saints?"

Sayyīdinā 'Alī ؎ said, "One of the most difficult is *ihtimālu 'l-adhā*, to carry peoples' harms."

What is their harm? It is not that they speak bad about the *walī*, like today they say that there are no *awlīyā*; rather, it is for the shaykh to carry the harm, the mistakes and the sins of his followers, and clean them by taking their mistakes on his shoulders and giving them from his good deeds and good tidings that he dressed them with. He is sacrificing himself for the benefit of his followers. That is a *walī's* job and that is a *walī,* what he gave him from the beginning.

And so when Sayyīdinā Mūsā ﷺ asked Sayyīdinā Khiḍr ﷺ, "Can I follow you?" he said, "Yes, but you have to be patient. I am not going to expose my secrets and I am carrying the harm and difficulty, taking into consideration my prophet will carry the burden and make people happy." That is why he took responsibility when he put a hole in the boat, as he didn't want the king to take the boat from the poor fisherman; then he took responsibility when he built the wall to save the treasure for its rightful heirs, and he took responsibility for that child that was harmful to his parents.

So our responsibility in *ṭarīqah* is to carry each other and not to criticize each other, and our way is not to advocate separation. And today all technology is the worst, as Mawlana said yesterday, because people are using it for destruction. You are destroying the morality of people on the Internet by saying things or showing things. And these three ways Allāh made under three actions. If you follow them, as Sayyīdinā ʿAlī ؓ said, Allāh will give you support, Prophet will give *shafāʿa,* and *awlīyā* will accept you as followers.

The first *ʿamal* is to do for *Ākhirah;* always do your best for the Hereafter, don't do the best for *dunyā. Man ʿamal li 'l-Ākhirah kafā-Allāhu dunyā hu,* "Whoever does his best for *Ākhirah,* Allāh will make people help him in *dunyā."* He doesn't need to work even, from everywhere help will come. If you are doing for Allāh ﷻ, Allāh will make people come to help you. But we are not doing enough for *Ākhirah* and that is why we are running after our *dunyā,* to be able to eat and drink!

And I can see and I observed and experienced how Mawlana Shaykh, may Allāh give him long life and may Allāh bless the soul of Grandshaykh, how they were only working for *daʿwah.* Allāh made people to come and serve them, their homes were never empty from anything. *SubhānAllāh*! Grandshaykh's home was so humble but three times a day food was served. If any guest came food was served and not one day there is no food in his house. *SubhānAllāh.* Allāh sent people to serve. And similarly with Mawlana Shaykh Nazim, may Allāh give him long life.

Grandshaykh ق one day said to me and my brother, "Who followed me, Allāh and Prophet promised to me in my visions, 'O ʿAbdAllāh Effendi! Anyone who follows you will not see *fi 'd-dunyā sharr aw fi 'l-Ākhirah,* never in *dunyā* will he see any harm and never in *Ākhirah,* and his pocket will never be empty of money.' Allāh gave every *walī* a specialty, anyone who follows me will never see harm in this life or the Next Life and their *rizq* will always be there." Their doors are always open and that is why whoever does for *Ākhirah,* Allāh will give him whatever he needs in *dunyā.*

Wa man aḥsana sarīratahu aḥsan Allāhu ẓāhirah, "The one who rides his ego and perfects his inside, Allāh will perfect his appearance." When he appears, any spot will be a spotlight, in any assembly or meeting or association, people will run to him because of that light that Allāh and his Prophet and *awlīyā* have put in his forehead. They run to him and they feel attracted like a magnet. That is why *awlīyāullāh* are like magnets; Allāh gave them that secret speciality. You cannot perfect your outside; that has to come from them. It is not perfecting outside by wearing nice clothes, but you need that heavenly light to be put and people will be attracted to that heavenly light.

So try to fix what is between you and people. These are major issues that if we follow, we succeed. *Awlīyā* succeeded, because they follow these ways. They began to know *ʿirfān,* Gnosticism. Allāh gave them the knowledge. They fixed that pipe between them and Allāh, and Allāh made people run to them!

May Allāh ﷻ forgive us and may Allāh ﷻ bless us.

Wa min Allāhi ʿt-tawfiq, bi ḥurmati ʿl-ḥabīb, bi ḥurmati ʿl-Fātiḥah.
And with Allāh is success. For the sake of the Beloved, for his sake we recite the opening chapter of Holy Qur'an.

Changeable and Unchangeable Principles

A'ūdhu billāhi min ash-Shayṭāni 'r-rajīm. Bismillāhi' r-Raḥmāni 'r-Raḥīm. Nawaytu 'l-arbā'īn, nawaytu 'l-'itikāf, nawaytu'l-khalwah, nawaytu 'l-'uzlah, nawaytu 'r-riyāḍa, nawaytu 's-sulūk, lillāhi Ta'alā fī hādhā 'l-masjid. Atī'ūllāha wa atī'ū 'r-Rasūla wa ūli 'l-amri minkum. (4:59)

Alhamdulillāh that Allāh ﷻ has connected us with people to whom He granted heavenly support. As followers or *murīds,* it is necessary for everyone, if he wants to find his journey and reach his goal, to know where he is putting his foot. To know where he is stepping, his intention has to be clean, that he is following the path of *Āhlu 's-Sunnah wa 'l-Jama'ah,* the path of *Āhlu 'l-Bayt,* and his intention has to be *Ṣādiq,* pure, on his journey. Because today people are connecting with so many *'ulamā* and different scholars, leaving the reality of Islam behind them and not giving importance to or even speaking about *Maqām al-Iḥsān,* the station where thoughts and characters are pure, and moral values are carried within you, which takes you to your goal and destiny.

Awlīyāullāh say that every person likes to reach somewhere. The goal is to reach Allāh's love and Prophet's love, but unfortunately, it is like a pipe with many holes, so water leaks through the holes and doesn't reach the end of the pipe, so you don't receive anything. *Qālū innamā kharam al-wusūl,* "They pierce their way by putting many holes in it," and they lost the *usūl,* the main principles of Islam, which is *Maqām al-Iḥsān.*

People say they want *Maqām al-Iḥsān,* but already they have put too many holes in their pipe, so how will they reach it? They will not. *Awlīyā* say you have to be careful. One of the big Sufi *'ālims,* Imām 'Abd al-Karīm ibn Hawāzin al-Qushayrī ق (d. 1074, Persia), said, "It is not good to follow someone who is not from this path (*Āhlu 's-Sunnah wa 'l-Jama'ah* and *Āhlu 'l-Bayt,* the Sufi path) as it might take you somewhere unaccepted. Today (700 years ago) people are on two ways and you have to avoid these two ways."

It means, not avoid them completely, but find someone who carries them and carries the reality of *Maqām al-Iḥsān.* "People today are people of footnotes and hearsay. They copy; they don't depend on what is new coming to hearts, refreshing their hearts. They copy what has been written, as this is their knowledge. They know what others wrote, but they don't progress to reach their destination. *aw imma aṣḥāb al-qawl wa 'l-fikr,* They are people of thoughts: academia and intellectuals. You have to be careful about them. They are thinking with the mind, and Allāh ﷻ cannot be known by the mind, He is known by hearts."

So today people copy and paste and if that knowledge is not footnoted, they don't accept it! So they copy what came before them or they use their mind to make "reforms," as if Islam needs reform. No, Islam doesn't need reform but Muslims need to reform, by returning to the tradition of Prophet ﷺ and his Companions ؓ! So the first group copy and paste and the second group are thinking people, like socialists who came at the beginning of the 20th century, Maududi, Syed Quṭb and many others, saying, "We have to reform Islam." No, you have to be very careful about what your mind is thinking.

Awlīyā take from the heart of Prophet ﷺ, and in that there are two principles: *thawābit*, firm, fixed elements that you cannot play with or change, and *mutaghayarāt,* changeable. The *thawābit* principles are not changed from copying and pasting, nor through academia thinking, but there has to be an inspiration from the heart of Prophet. Allāh ﷻ sends to Prophet, and Prophet sends to the hearts of *awlīyā*. This is why Jalāluddin Rumi ق brought so many changeable principles that he dressed on *thawābit,* firm principles, because firm principles can be dressed with whatever dress you like.

Allāh ﷻ is known through His Beautiful Names, so His Beautiful Names can be dressed. Allāh will manifest on His Prophet with His Beautiful Names, and He can dress on anyone from His Beautiful Names and grant them to know what name they are under. And there are many Names. Like *tajalli ʿIsmullāh al-ʿAẓam,* the Manifestation of the Name Encompassing all Names, "Allāh". How will it be manifested? For example, it will be manifested on "one," as in Holy Qur'an it is mentioned:

> *Wa annahu lamma qāma ʿabdullāhi yadʿūhu kādū yakūnūna ʿalayhi libada.*
> *Yet when the Devotee of Allāh stands forth to invoke Him, they just make round him a dense crowd.* (Sūrat al-Jinn, 72:19)

When Allāh's servant, the only one mentioned in Holy Qur'an as "ʿAbdAllāh'," which means He dressed Prophet ﷺ with His Beautiful Names and with *ʿIsmullāh al-ʿAẓam,* the Name encompassing all the Beautiful Names and Attributes, "Allāh".

Prophet ﷺ is the only one on whom Allāh ﷻ manifested His Beautiful Names and Attributes, because he reached the highest rank and highest *shān*, prestige, the reality and certainty of the manifestation of His Highest Beautiful Name, "Allāh". That is why he was able to go in *'Isrā wal-Mi'rāj*. If Allāh ﷻ did not dress him, he would have been completely annihilated! Allāh dressed him so he can come back. So Imām al-Qushayrī ق said, "When the servant of Allāh asks through prayers, that Name was for Prophet and his inheritors," who are *Ghawth, Aqtāb, Budalā, Nujabā, Nuqabā, Awtād, Akhyār.*

So the reality is not changeable. They can be dressed by *mutaghayarāt,* changeable principles, and in this way you can give every reality a colorful dress that you can follow. He continues:

> *Wa law istaqāmū 'alā aṭ-ṭariqati lā asqaynāhum mā'an ghadaqa.*
> *If they kept straight forward on the way, ṭarīqah, we would shower them with blessings.*

"If they stay on the Way, *Ṣirāṭ al-Mustaqīm,*" this is a fixed principle. But you can dress that principle, that anyone can go on that path, in a different manifestation, with different dresses, with different shuyūkh, with different *dhikr*. The road doesn't change, but your technique as you go from one shaykh to another is a dress that can be changed. Allāh said in Holy Qur'an: *wa law istaqāmū 'alā aṭ-ṭariqati lā asqaynāhum mā'an ghadaqa.*

Today they know now where rain comes from and to where it goes. The reality of the rain doesn't change. There are lakes or equatorial areas to where water evaporates, that is unchangeable, but where that rain is sent is changeable.

> *Wal baladu 'ṭ-ṭayyibu yakhruju nabātuhu bi-idhni rabbihi wa'Lladhī khabutha lā yakhruju illa nakidan kadhālika nuṣarrifu 'l-ayāti li-qawmin yashkurūn.*
> *From the land that is clean and good, by the will of its Cherisher, springs up produce, (rich) after its kind, but from the land that is bad, springs up nothing but that which is begrudging. Thus do we explain the signs by various (symbols) to those who are grateful.* (Sūrat al-A'rāf, 7:58)

The clouds are there, but Allāh ﷻ moves them as He likes by wind, which is in hands of angels, which is changeable. The principles of evaporation are unchangeable. For example, if you drop water on the floor, in ten or fifteen minutes it evaporates. If you go to the sauna, you sweat. Similarly, you have to sweat in the way of *ṭarīqah*. If you don't sweat, what is the benefit? Do you want to sit on the throne and for them to carry you? *nuqsānīyyah,* you have deficiencies they must work on for you to improve. For example, you don't like watermelon, so they give you watermelon; that is a bitterness, a sweat. This one likes to sleep too much, so they keep him awake! So everyone has to sweat and in a different way.

"I Am not Worthy to See Allah"

So a big *walī* said to someone who is higher than him but he didn't know, and *awlīyā* like to joke with each other, "Do you like to see Him, *aturīdu an tarāh.*" The same question applies to everyone here: do you like to see Him? Yes, of course! Why are you coming to make *dhikrūllāh*? To see Him, to be more near Him. That *walī* answered, "No, I don't like to see Him."

If they ask us, we would run to see Him! Sayyīdinā Mūsā ﷺ asked to see Him! So this *walī* was careful and so he said no. They said that is strange.

He continued, *unnaziḥu dhāk al-Jamāl ʿan nadhari mithlih,* "I exalt that Beauty from Someone who has my eyes," meaning, "I am not worthy; I don't want my dirty eyes to see that Beauty, because that Beauty is exalted." To see that Beauty requires clean eyes. Can we say that?

They said, "When do you relax?" Today they say when you relax, take a massage. (laughter)

He said, "No, *mā dumtu lahu dhākiran,* as long as I am remembering Him, I am relaxing. When I am heedless from His remembrance, I will not find any relaxation; I am sweating."

So you see the difference between them and us? Imām al-Qushayrī ق said, *wa law istaqāmūʿalā at-ṭarīqati lā asqaynahum mā'an ghadaqa,* "If they knew the variants (*utaghayarāt*), they would have succeeded."

Light is a constant speed, traveling at 300,000 Km/s. The moon has many variations in density between it and Earth; that is *mutaghayarāt*. That is why the speed of light coming from the moon is less than 300,000 Km/s, as there is a lot of friction taking place within that distance. So in this galaxy with so many stars—some farther than the moon, the sun, or the polestar—your destination on this path is farther than any star in this universe. And a lot of variations might drop your power to move forward. That is why the guide will teach you what *awrād* to say, to make you move depending on your capacity. If you connect a 500-watt lamp to a 100-watt power source, the light, the lamp, and the wire will burn. But if you connect a 50-watt lamp to a 100-watt power source, neither the lamp nor the wire will burn. So the shaykh knows the capacity your heart can carry; he connects you, and your light is not burned out, and you move on that path. What the shaykh gives is *mutaghayarāt,* something that changes. He might give you a 50-watt or a 100-watt connection.

So Allāh ﷻ said in Holy Qur'an, "If he would stand on the path, we would order angels to send these clouds of mercy and put in their hearts. We would shower them with 'un-understandables' (unique knowledge)."

Support comes from Allāh ﷻ. If you are on a track ready to move, as you are given awrād from your shaykh and you do it, then mercy, *ināyatullāh,* comes to push you like the wind blowing the clouds of rain. That is *rīḥ aṣ-ṣibā,* "cool breeze from Heavens" that moves you forward. Like a carriage on a track only needs the first push and it keeps going like a roller coaster. It might find a hill but it will go slowly up and then will go down quickly.

Allāh ﷻ said, *inna maʿ al-ʿusri yusrā,* "With difficulty comes ease." (94:6) He didn't say, "With ease comes difficulty," no, with difficulty there must be ease. So you face difficulty first, then you reach ease, as Allāh ﷻ confirmed:

Alam nashraḥ laka saḍrak, wa wadāʿnā ʿanka wizrak.
Have We not opened your breast for you and removed from you your burden.
(Sūrat al-Shahr, 94:1-2)

Then, when you are steady on path, He sends angels to move these clouds of mercy and you quickly reach your goal. Today people are so interested in *an-naql wa 'l-athar,* "This one said this and this one said that." If you don't say the transmission of that knowledge, it is not acceptable. But everything is changeable, as today there are *awlīyāullāh* inspired from the heart of Prophet ﷺ, who said, "I left behind the Book of Allāh and my Way," and, "I left behind the Book and my Family."

Put these two different *ḥadīth* in an equation with the first side *kitābullāh wa sunnatī — kitābullāh wa ʿitratī.* Remove what is common on both sides, *kitābullāh,* so what is left? *Sunnatī —ʿItratī.* So you have to look, those who are on his way are from his Family. Who are his Family? Many are from his blood family and also there is his spiritual family, like Sayyīdinā Salmān al-Fārsi ؓ. *Awlīyā* are the ones who can take you forward to understand *kitābullāh,* the Book of Allāh. Others only say, "He said this and he said that," but they do not understand what is coming new. That is *ʿilm al-ghuyūb* for you, but for them that is *ʿilm aẓ-ẓuhūr,* knowledge appearing for them.

So follow those who are receiving divine inspiration in their hearts, *shuyūkh aṭ-ṭā'ifah,* shaykhs of that particular group. Who are they? They are *awlīyāullāh.* If you follow others, you are in a maze. So *awlīyā* take you out of that maze. *Awlīyāullāh* are all on the similar way. Think-tank intellectuals believe if they study four years, they become a doctor and put that certificate. No, *awlīyā* are those who take you through your life, the past, future and present, giving you precisely what you need at any given moment. Now the intellectuals are coming to reform Islam. Islam is perfect like the full moon! You cannot reform Islam with ideas of Marx, Lenin, or socio-political movements such as communism, socialism, or even democratic or liberal ideologies. You have to come with something that is more spiritual and in the middle, which everyone can follow.

So Prophet ﷺ mentioned in many *aḥadīth,* and what is revealed in Holy Qur'an, that the best way to reach that is through *dhikrūllāh* and different ways of *dhikr*. Allāh ﷻ describes Himself for us with Ninety-nine Beautiful Names. You can go to infinite Names to remember Him and you have to know the highest is *ʿIsmullāh,* "Allāh," and when the servant of Allāh ﷻ stood up to pray, he is the one whom Allāh ﷻ dressed with all the Beautiful Names and Attributes. Abdus-Salām is under the *tajallī* of the Divine Name "as-Salām," but "ʿAbdAllāh," Allāh's Servant, is under the *tajallī* of all the Beautiful Names and Attributes!

So *awlīyā* are changeable, based on what is dressing them, so may Allāh ﷻ clean us with His endless power! Be careful about that verse, *wa law istaqāmū ʿalā aṭ-ṭarīqati la asqaynāhum mā'an ghadaqa.*

May Allāh ﷻ fill our hearts with all His Names and Attributes. May Allāh ﷻ forgive us and may Allāh ﷻ bless us.

Wa min Allāhi ʿt-tawfiq, bi ḥurmati ʿl-ḥabīb, bi ḥurmati ʿl-Fātiḥah.
And with Allāh is success. For the sake of the Beloved, for his sake we recite the opening chapter of Holy Qur'an.

Dhikrullah Is the Main Pillar of Tariqah

A'ūdhu billāhi min ash-Shayṭāni 'r-rajīm. Bismillāhi' r-Raḥmāni 'r-Raḥīm. Nawaytu 'l-arbā'īn, nawaytu 'l-'itikāf, nawaytu'l-khalwah, nawaytu 'l-'uzlah, nawaytu 'r-riyāḍa, nawaytu 's-sulūk, lillāhi Ta'ālā fī hādhā 'l-masjid. Atī'ūllāha wa atī'ū 'r-Rasūla wa ūli 'l-amri minkum. (4:59)

R*ābiṭah* is the connection of the pipe from you to the shaykh. When he takes your hand for initiation, he is connecting you. In the same way you connect a pipe with fittings, he connects all the fittings so there is no leak. And not only does he connect the fittings, but he glues them also so it will never break. So always the *rābiṭah* is the connection with fittings and it is glued so that it is never going to break. And *murāqabah* is to keep observing both from the *walī's*/shaykh's side and from the *murīd's* side. From both sides they are always in observation. *Murāqabah* means to observe like a video camera what is going on, to be vigilant to maintain that pipe with no leakage.

As a *murīd*, from your side you are looking to make sure that if there is a defect you fix it, and from the side of the shaykh, he is looking for any defects to fix. If you want to count the defects between you and your shaykh, you can realize there are a lot of holes and leaks in that pipe and nothing can fix them except heavenly glue; you can't use *dunyā* glue or anything else as it will not work. Heavenly glue is *dhikrūllāh*, and that heavenly backbone or pillar on which you can lean is *dhikrūllāh*.

To do *dhikrūllāh*, you have to be clean. When you do *dhikr* it means you are knocking on the door to be opened for you. Allāh ﷻ said in Holy Qur'an:

> *Alladhīna yadhkurūnullāh qiyamān wa qu'ūdan wa 'alā junūbihim wa yattafakkarūna fī khalqi 's-samāwātī wa 'l-arḍ, rabbanā mā khalaqta hadhā bāṭilan subḥānaka fa qinā 'adhāba 'n-nār.*
> *Those who remember Allāh (always, and in prayers) standing, sitting, and lying down on their sides, and think deeply about the Creation of the Heavens and the Earth, (saying),"Our Lord! You have not created (all) this without purpose, glory to You! Give us salvation from the torment of the Fire.*
>
> (Sūrat 'Āli 'Imrān, 3:191)

Al-ladhīna yadhkurūnullāh, "Those who mention their Creator, Allāh ﷻ, on their tongues in different ways and positions." So when you mention Allāh ﷻ, you go into that pillar of *ṭarīqah. Ṭarīqah* doesn't differ from Sharīʿah. Sharīʿah is the law and *ṭarīqah* is the way. You cannot change what Allāh ﷻ has ordered for us, the law of Islam, the obligations. *Imān,* what the Prophet ﷺ described, you cannot change. You cannot change the constitution Allāh ﷻ gave to Muslims; the Holy Qur'an and the Holy Ḥadīth of Prophet cannot be changed!

Ṭarīqah is the way to execute these laws. One of the main pillars of *ṭarīqah* is *dhikrūllāh,* and Allāh mentioned, "The best of *dhikr* is to know *lā ilāha illa-Llāh,* which is *Maqām at-Tawḥīd,* the Station of Oneness of Being." So to glue and restore what is broken, you have to come back to *dhikrūllāh.* I'm not speaking of *dhikrūllāh* that is a public association, but rather *dhikrūllāh* when you are alone, as Prophet mentioned, *ijʿal lisānak ratban bi dhikrūllāh,* "Keep your tongue wet with *dhikrūllāh.*"

How are we spending our time, in *dhikrūllāh* or in *dhikr ad-dunyā,* in Allāh's remembrance or in remembrance of *dunyā?* As soon as you remember *dunyā,* you need *ghusl* (prescribed shower of purification). You cannot come to Allāh's door bringing your *dunyā* with you! That is *adab at-ṭarīqah,* "principles of *ṭarīqah.*" You cannot come to an association of *dhikrūllāh* with no *ghusl.* That is why Sayyīdinā Shah Naqshband ق didn't allow any of his followers in his time to attend his sessions without not only *wuḍū,* but a complete *ghusl.* Do you know why you are required to make *ghusl* after you and your wife are intimate? It is not only to remove *najāsah* (impurity); that act is pure, clean. But you make *ghusl,* saying, "*Yā Rabbī*! I am moving from the desire you put in me for my family to my desire for You." That is why the curtain between you and Allāh ﷻ is very thin. So when you are in *dunyā* and you fulfill Allāh's order, you take *ghusl* when you finish (that act), in order to go back to Allāh's remembrance and open that door.

Al-Qushayrī ؓ, one of the biggest scholars of *taṣawwuf,* said, *Lam adkhul fī ḥudūri 'sh-shaykh illa ṣā'iman mughtasilan,* "I never enter the presence of my shaykh without having taken a shower and observing fast, and whenever I come to his school, I enter, go to the door of the place where he is sitting, and then I back up, respecting him, not coming inside with my ego or my *dunyā* because I am worried."

Today, how do we go to the door of the shaykh? What determines who goes in and who stays out? Who pays more money is allowed in!

Imām Al-Qushayrī ؓ continues, "If I have the courage and insist to enter, then as soon as I enter I feel numb from the *tajallī*, divine manifestations, coming on my shaykh that make me run away trembling."

This is the beginning of the journey. We are lucky because we are in a time that is full of ignorance. As Grandshaykh ق said, that is why Allāh ﷻ opened more and more His doors of mercy. Because of these doors of mercy there is no more protocol, no more this discipline that is a prerequisite. Like a child that is spoiled, does he have any kind of principles to enter his father's room? Even if his father is president or king, no one will stop him and he enters. We are spoiled today with that *raḥmat* opening from Allāh ﷻ and there are no more restrictions.

So *awlīyāullāh* no longer look at the behavior of their followers; they say, "That is okay." Before, they could not take a step, out of respect and discipline toward the shaykh; a student became numb and went back. Today, no one is asking because of that huge *tajallī* of mercy coming on *Ummat an-Nabī* and on this *dunyā*. When you have a lot of water, you can use it in any way you like, even for irrigation of crops, but if you don't have water you save it. The *awlīyāullāh* used to save the *raḥmat* for their followers, but now it is coming like an ocean. So let them take it; with that *raḥmat* they will be blessed and cleaned.

So if al-Qushayrī ؓ said, "I would not enter my teacher's presence without fasting or taking a shower," oh *murīd*, how then do you dare to knock on the door of Allāh, which is *dhikrūllāh*? How can you go there without fasting from not only food, but also from all desires? You must come clean. As soon as you sit in the association of *dhikrūllāh*, your thoughts interfere and take you right and left, so Allāh ﷻ made *dhikrūllāh* an obligation.

> *Yā ayyuha 'Lladhīna āmanū 'dhkurūllāha dhikran kathīra wa sabiḥūhu bukratan wa aṣīla. Hūwa 'Lladhī yuṣalli 'alaykum wa malā'ikatahu li yukhrijakum min aẓ-ẓulumāti ila 'n-nūr.*
> *O you who believe! Remember Allāh! Continue to mention Him without limit, before sunrise and before sunset. He is The One Who encourages, appreciates, and supports you all, and His angels, and replaces darkness and tyranny with divine Light.* (Sūrat al-'Aḥzāb, 33:41-43)

This means *dhikr* not only by tongue, but with all your senses, all your organs, all your body, all your soul and with everything possible to use that Allāh ﷻ has given you! You have to mention and continue reciting, not His Name, but entering the Ocean of Vision and seeing defects in your body and soul, and enter to that Presence. Mention to yourself, don't mention to people. *Dhikrun kathīra* means "excessive *dhikr*". How do we do *dhikr?* For ten or fifteen minutes only, but *dhikrun kathīra* has no end; it is non-stopping, a continuous remembrance of Allāh ﷻ, in your day and night! So if you stop, you are coming against His will.

That is the difference between *awlīyāullāh* and people; they are in constant *dhikrūllāh*, while we do *dhikr* for one hour and stop. Their hearts are constantly in remembrance. *kathīra* means, "unlimited". Then, *sabihū bukratan wa aṣīlā*. So first is *dhikrūllāh*, because as Allāh ﷻ said, "And We are nearer to him than his jugular vein." (al-Qaf, 50:16). It means, "Don't leave My Presence!" Allāh is possessive of His servant: He doesn't like the heart of His servant to be occupied or possessed except by Him. So Allāh ﷻ wants *awlīyāullāh* to be exclusively for Him.

> *Qulnā 'hbiṭū minhā jamī'an fa imma yātīyannakum minnī hudan faman tabi'a hudāya fa lā khawfun 'alayhim wa lā hum yaḥzanūn.*
> *We said, "All of you get down from here, and if, as is sure, there comes to you guidance from Me, whosoever follows My guidance, on them shall be no fear, nor shall they grieve.* (Sūrat al-Baqarah, 2:38)

Awlīyāullāh never feel sad because Allāh is taking care of them, making them slaves at His door. So there is a huge gap (in conduct) for *murīds* to be at the door of their teacher.

Wadhkurullāha dhikran kathīra wa sabihūhu bukratan wa asīla, "And praise him and glorify him morning and evening." There is morning remembrance and evening remembrance.

> *Yā ayyuha 'Lladhīna āmanū 'dhkurullāha dhikran kathīra wa sabihūhu bukratan wa asīla. Hūwa 'Lladhī yusalli 'alaykum li yukhrijakum min adh-dhulumāti ila 'n-nūr.*
> *O you who believe! Remember Allāh! Continue to mention Him without limit, before sunrise and before sunset. He is The One Who encourages, appreciates, and supports you all, and replaces darkness and tyranny with divine Light.*
> (Sūrat al-'Aḥzāb, 33:41-43)

The Pillar of Tariqah

That is *'imād at-ṭarīqah,* the "Pillar of *Ṭarīqah.*" Then Allāh brings you to His Presence after you do that continuous remembrance and glorify Him morning and evening, then what? Allāh and His angels will send blessings on you. *Inna Allāha wa malā'ikatahu yuṣallūn,* He will raise you to be connected to the heart of Sayyīdinā Muḥammad ﷺ; as He orders his angels to send blessing on Prophet, He also orders His angels to send blessings on you, to take you up, away from darkness to light. What darkness? Darkness of *dunyā,* which for *awlīyā* is not worth anything. That is why they became ascetics; they left *dunyā* and those who took it made a mistake. Our duty is to leave the desires of *dunyā,* but if Allāh makes *dunyā* a slave running after you, that is no problem.

Hūwa 'Lladhī yuṣalli 'alaykum wa malā' ikatahu li yukhrijakum min aẓ-ẓulumāti ila 'n-nūr. "He is The One Who supports you and takes you from darkness to light." When He takes you from darkness to light, *wa kān bil-mu'minīna Raḥīmā.* "He is showing you His mercy." It means, "You remember Me! I am ordering My angels to pray on you, and send that mercy on you."

So when *awlīyā* see this, they insist *dhikrūllāh* is the pillar of *ṭarīqah.* They don't ask people to do *irshād,* which is not for everyone, but they tell them do *dhikr* so they will benefit.

And Prophet ﷺ said:

Yā 'ibn ādam idhā dhakartanī faqad shakartanī kathīran wa idhā nasītanī kafarta, wa bish-shukru tadūm an-ni'am.
O son of Adam! If you mention Me, it means you are thanking Me. By thanking Allāh, favors will not stop reaching you.

And Prophet ﷺ said in a Holy *Hadīth*:

O son of Adam! If you mention Me you are thanking Me, and if you thank someone he gives you more.

What do you think of Allāh ﷻ? If you thank Him, you get more, so to remember Him is to thank Him. *Wa idhā nasītanī kafarta.* "And if you stopped remembering Me, you are not becoming an unbeliever." *Kuffār* here does not mean "unbeliever," but rather "to make a mistake," or, "You have ignored My favors on you."

When you don't thank who is generous with you, what will he say? It means you didn't care, you are ungrateful. Here *kafartanī* means "ungrateful"; it does not mean "to become non-Muslim". You are ungrateful when you forget Him, so show gratitude to Allāh!

Prophet ﷺ said:

Khayru 'l-ʿamal dhikrūllāh.
The best of deeds is to remember Allāh.

Wa qāl an-nabī li kulli shay'in saqālan wa saqāl al-qulūb dhikrūllāh.
For everything there is a polish and polish of the heart is dhikrūllāh.

Like a diamond is in a rock, and to take it out you must cut the rock and then you polish it. The shaykh polishes us like a rock. Many of us go to the shaykh as tyrants, so what does he do? He has to break you down and hammer on you. They ask, "Why is Shaykh hammering on me?" Because he loves you, and that is to help you. When he shouts at you, don't get upset because he is carrying your problems! For everything there is polish and the best polish for hearts is *dhikrūllāh.*

Prophet ﷺ said:

O my Companions! If you find Riyāḍ al-Jannah, the Heavenly Gardens on Earth, stay there and sit in it and be in it. They asked, "Are there heavenly gardens on Earth?" He said, "Yes, the associations of dhikrūllāh."

It means *dhikrūllāh* of Holy Qur'an, Holy Hadith, the Beautiful Names and Attributes, or of holy prophets. So when you find such associations, go and sit in them as that is Heaven on Earth.

Do you want Heaven on Earth? People go everywhere looking for Heaven on Earth. Go sit with humble, broken-hearted people: sit with people of *dhikrūllāh*. That is what we need. We don't need to sit with presidents or kings. They are leaving whatever they have behind them (when they die). Those sitting in *dhikrūllāh* sessions are finding Heaven on Earth, where they clean their hearts for their Lord, then receive these manifestations.

Wa qīla man kāna yurīd an yaʿrif manzilatahu ʿindallāh fal yanẓur ilā manzilatillāhu fī qalbih. "As much as we are keeping Allāh in our hearts, Allāh is keeping us." Say the truth: who are we keeping more in our hearts, Allāh or our children? We are always keeping our children in our hearts.

One of the *awlīyāullāh*, Abū ʿAlī ad-Daqāq ق, said, *"Dhikrūllāh* is *manshūr al-wilāyah*, the proclamation of sainthood." That big proclamation is displayed everywhere, and throughout circles of *dhikr* they know you are a *walī*. Your level can be known there, because you are from ʿAbdal, Nujabā, Nuqabā, Awtād, Akhyār, and Quṭb, Quṭb al-Bilād, Quṭb al-Aqtāb, Quṭb al-Irshād, Quṭb al-Mutaṣarrif. Everyone knows his level. *wa man utīyya dhālika al-manshūr...* "And whoever keeps his *dhikr* has that proclamation," and who has been *sulib,* one who *dhikrūllāh* has been taken from his heart, that means he has been "laid off", he is no more in that heavenly gathering on Earth.

And it is said *dhikrūllāh* is better than *fikr,* to think. With thinking you have to pull information or knowledge, and with your mind you can only pull *dunyā* knowledge, you cannot pull secrets. However, with *dhikr Allāh* ﷻ opens for you the interpretation of Holy Qur'an and the Holy Hadith, and an understanding of what *awlīyā* have said. *Allāh taʿalā yuṣaf bihi wa lā yuṣaf bil-fikr, "Allāh* ﷻ is not described by thought, but He is described by remembering Him." A mental description is too limited.

Grandshaykh ق said, "The punishment of a *walī* is to be cut from *dhikr,"* because Allāh said:

F'adhkurūnī adhkurkum.
Remember Me and I remember you; mention Me and I mention you.
(Sūrat al-Baqarah, 2:152)

O students of Mawlana Shaykh Nazim ق! We are lucky and blessed to be connected to such a *walī,* who is connected to the Golden Chain through two big oceans, Sayyīdinā Abū Bakr aṣ-Ṣiddīq ق and Sayyīdinā ʿAlī ﷺ, *maraj al-baḥrayn yaltaqiyyān,* "two oceans coming together and between them is a thin divider." Those are two places of knowledge that come together, as mentioned in Sūrat ar-Raḥmān, that He made the two oceans come together with very thin divider between them.

Maraja al-baḥrayni yaltaqiyāni baynahumā barzakhun lā yabghīyān.
He has let loosed the two seas meeting together. Between them is a barrier which none of them can transgress. (Sūrat ar-Raḥmān, 55:19-20)

That is the *baḥr,* ocean, of Sayyīdinā Abū Bakr and the *baḥr* of Sayyīdinā ʿAli! The two of them came together in Sayyīdinā Jafar aṣ-Ṣadiq ق. May Allāh bless these two great ones and all *Ṣaḥābah* ﷺ of Prophet ﷺ and His deputies ق, and those looking for normal life, not a life of extremism!

May Allāh ﷻ forgive us and may Allāh ﷻ bless us.

Wa min Allāhi 't-tawfiq, bi ḥurmati 'l-ḥabīb, bi ḥurmati 'l-Fātiḥah.
And with Allāh is success. For the sake of the Beloved, for his sake we recite the opening chapter of Holy Qur'an.

Characteristics and Levels of Dhikrullah

A'ūdhu billāhi min ash-Shayṭāni 'r-rajīm. Bismillāhi' r-Raḥmāni 'r-Raḥīm. Nawaytu 'l-arbā'īn, nawaytu 'l-'itikāf, nawaytu'l-khalwah, nawaytu 'l-'uzlah, nawaytu 'r-riyāḍa, nawaytu 's-sulūk, lillāhi Ta'alā fi hādhā 'l-masjid. Atī'ūllāha wa atī'ū 'r-Rasūla wa ūli 'l-amri minkum. (4:59)

Every one of us intend to love Allāh ﷻ, our Prophet ﷺ, our shaykh ق, and to love everyone. But we are weak servants, *pas faible, très faible;* we cannot do more than what we are doing. However, it is nice to know what *awlīyāullāh* think of those things we are heedless about. Their knowledge is very high and ours is very limited.

The Prophet ﷺ said:

Innamā al-'amālu bin-niyyāt wa innamā li-kulli 'mrin mā nawā.
Every action is by intention and truly to every man is what he intended.
(Bukhari and Muslim)

We were speaking in the previous session about the importance of *dhikrūllāh,* which is important for everyone seeking this path. *Shuyukh aṭ-ṭā'ifa,* which means, "shaykhs of *taṣawwuf*", all of them with their differences and different ways of *dhikrūllāh.* As much as there are differences in that Way it is better, because people are able to find and take from the tap that quenches their thirst. This one makes *dhikr* in this way, this one in that way. It is okay as all of them are making *dhikr* to The One, Whom you cannot describe, the Exalted One. You cannot describe Him through any kind of thoughts in your mind. *Lā yaṣifahu bil-fikr.* "You cannot describe Allāh ﷻ through your mind." Only through what Allāh describes Himself you can understand, through His Beautiful Names and Attributes. But you cannot understand the Essence.

Awlīyāullāh are swimming in these oceans to pull out these treasures, and the deeper they go the deeper the water becomes and they cannot reach (an end). *Kullamā taqarabū wajad al-masāfa ab'ad.* "However nearer they come, the distance increases and to pass it is difficult." In the *Mi'rāj,* Prophet Muḥammad ﷺ reached *Qāba Qawsayni aw Adnā,* very near, *"two bows' length or nearer."* But with that nearness which is only for Prophet, it is still far to reach the Reality of Allāh's Essence. No one can reach that! How far is the

Divine Presence? Only Prophet knows, but the Essence is much further (beyond that).

That is why Allāh ﷻ is always putting different meanings in the heart of Prophet ﷺ and in the hearts of *awlīyāullāh*. That is why ascensions never end.

Wa fawqa kull dhi ʿilmin ʿalīm.
Above every knower is a (higher) knower. (Sūrat Yūsuf, 12:76)

This *ayah* also means that in every moment there is a higher knowledge (revealed). That is why books contain knowledge of the past and knowledge of that time, when written by *awlīyā*, but tomorrow a higher knowledge will be revealed. Grandshaykh ق said, "In the time of Sayyīdinā Mahdī ؑ, if you open any book there will be nothing in it; all the writing will have disappeared." All previous knowledge will have passed, but in the time of Sayyīdinā Mahdī ؑ there is new knowledge called, *khāmis al-Qur'an*, "the secret of the Qur'an."

Today no secret of the Qur'an comes out, but then that secret with 12,000-to-24,000 oceans of knowledge will come on every letter of Qur'an to hearts of seekers! Those living in that time will immediately understand and reach their destiny in sainthood.

(An attendee sneezes.) Yarḥamakullāh. I did not hear you say, '*Alḥamdulillāh*', which is a sin, and we are witness on that. *(Attendee says, "Alḥamdulillāh!")* When someone sneezes, you must say *'Alḥamdulillāh'* and then we respond, *'yarḥamakullāh'*. If he does not say that, we are not responsible to reply. Allāh ﷻ said:

Fadhkurūnī adhkurkum, wa ashkurū lī wa lā takfurūna.
Remember Me and I will remember you, and thank Me and don't be ungrateful. (Sūrat al-Baqarah, 2:152)

That specialty is only for *Ummat an-Nabī*. Before, for other nations, it was *adhkurūnī*, "Remember Me." But for *Ummat an-Nabī*, Allāh ﷻ added, *adhkurkum*, "I remember you." Others are under the order to remember Him, what He revealed in another verse:

Utlu mā uḥīyya ilayk min al-kitābi wa aqimi 'ṣ-ṣalāta inna'ṣ-ṣalāta tanhā ʿani'l-faḥshāi wa 'l-munkari wa ladhikrullāhi akbaru w'Allāhu yʿalamu mā taṣnaʿūn.

Recite what is sent of the Book by inspiration to you, and establish regular prayer, for prayer restrains from shameful and unjust deeds. And remembrance of Allāh is the greatest (thing in life) without doubt. And Allāh knows the (deeds) you do. (Sūrat al-ʿAnkabūt, 29:45)

Allāh's remembrance is for *Ummat an-Nabī,* but His mentioning of you is higher and greater. How much higher and greater? There is no limit in that greatness! That means in every moment, even if you remember Him one moment in your life, you are *ʿabd,* servant, and your *ʿibādah,* worship, is limited. So if you mentioned Him one time in your life, saying, "*Yā Allāh*!" or, "*lā ilāha illa-Llāh,*" Allāh will render it back to you non-stop until the Day of Judgment, and He will assign angels to send praise on you non-stop, without end and with no limits! That is for one time, and it is enough for Allāh ﷻ to send in every moment! Let us say now, *Yā Rabb*! *Yā Rabb*! O Allāh! O Allāh! That is for you a great blessing.

That is why the association of *dhikr* is a light, as angels are there. It becomes a place of *ʿibādah,* worshipness. Allāh ﷻ is looking and that place becomes a place of worshipness, where angels are all the time. That is why they say to appoint in your home a place only for prayers and *ṣalawāt*. To enter there has to be with *adab,* discipline. You cannot enter there in your normal daily life, as that area becomes special and it has heavenly visitors.

That is why Sayyida Maryam's place became sacred. *Kullamā dakhala ʿalayha zakarīyya 'l-miḥrāb wajada ʿindahā rizqā*. Whenever Sayyīdinā Zakarīya ﷺ entered that place, he found provision there. So there, he asked Allāh to give him a child, and Allāh ﷻ granted him Sayyīdinā Yaḥyā ﷺ. So it is nice to have *makān al-ibadah,* a place of worship, and later it becomes a *Maqām al-ʿIbādah,* a place of worship where manifestations of angels come on you; angels must be present there.

One of *awlīyāullāh* said, *law lā anna dhikrūllāh taʿalā farḍan lamā dhakartuhu ijlālan lahu.* "If it was not an obligation to remember Allāh, to mention His Beautiful Names and Attributes, or to mention Him in recitation of Holy Qur'an, I would never do it."

It is ordered in the verse of *dhikr* mentioned previously; there might be 50-60 *ayāt* in Holy Qur'an. If it was not an order he will not mention it! Why? This is very significant.

He said, "How do I mention Him?" as when you mention Him you are entering the Divinely Presence. "How am I mentioning His Majesty when I revere Him so much, *ijlālan.* How can someone weak mention Someone

Who created him? I feel ashamed. I have to wash my mouth before I open it *alfu alfu*, a thousand by a thousand (1,000 x 1,000) times of repentance." That means, "Millions of repentances I have to do before I open my mouth to remember Him!"

Today when we come to *dhikr*, we come lazy. Why lazy? Because according to that *walī*, our soul knows that we are weak and our soul is ashamed from the doings of our bodies, which always contradict whatever Allāh wants, so we do the opposite. Our body is absorbed in *dunyā* desire and our soul is absorbed in heavenly desire. So when you come for *dhikrūllāh*, be sure you are very clean. As we said, in previous times they came to *dhikr* only in pure white clothes reserved for that. They had a room to change into their very clean clothes, with no dust. Today they say there are no special requirements, that to just attend *dhikr* is enough. Allāh's mercy is in this time (and standards have dropped).

They asked one person, *a'anta ṣāimun,* "Are you fasting?"

He said, *naʿm anā ṣāimun bi dhikrillāh.* "Yes, I am fasting, as I am remembering Him, making *dhikrūllāh* in every moment. I am not with you, I am in the Divine Presence with My Lord. If I remember anyone other than My Lord, then I break fast."

Not like us; we say we are fasting if we are not eating. Let's count in 24 hours, how much we are mentioning Allāh's Name and how much we are mentioning each other's names? It might be that in 23 hours and 59 minutes we are mentioning *dunyā,* and the rest is mentioning and remembering Allāh, our Creator, and that we are His weak servants (*i.e.,* one minute)!

And a *jawāriḥ* (whose limbs do *dhikrūllāh*) mentioned, "There was a man between us who says *'Allāh, Allāh,'* and one day a tree branch fell on his head and split it open. (There were no stitches at that time to close the wound) and blood was running from his head and gushed on the ground, and it began to write *'Allāh, Allāh.'*" That one was mentioning Allāh 23 hours and 59 minutes, because with him everything was with *dhikrūllāh.*

Also, there was a lady in Egypt who died recently. She never answered any question except with a verse of Holy Qur'an; even she wanted to eat, from Qur'an she mentioned foods and they prepared that food for her. She didn't eat anything that is not mentioned in Holy Qur'an. Allāh mentions in Qur'an that He made *halāl* for you *ibil* and other kinds of meats, and birds, and fruits of the sea. Always she answered from Holy Qur'an and never she opened her mouth to answer from other than that, until she died! Where are such people today?

Previous nations were prescribed *dhikr* at certain times, but *Ummat an-Nabī* was granted to make *dhikr* at any time, in their heart or by tongue. Allāh ﷻ said in Holy Qur'an:

> *Al-ladhīna yadhkurūnallāh qīyāman wa quʿūdān wa ʿalā junūbīhim wa yattafakkarūna fi khalqi 's-samāwātī wa 'l-arḍ, rabbanā mā khalaqta hadha bāṭilan subḥānaka fa qinā ʿadhāba 'n-nār.*
>
> *Those who remember Allāh (always, and in prayers) standing, sitting, and lying down on their sides, and who think deeply about the Creation of the Heavens and the Earth, (saying), "Our Lord! You have not created (all) this without purpose. Glory to You! Give us salvation from the torment of the Fire."* (Sūrat 'Āli 'Imrān, 3:191)

And there is *dhikr* of the heart, *dhikr* of the tongue, and *dhikr* of the soul. When the heart and tongue *dhikr* coincide, that is an opening for the soul to remember Allāh, as in 24 hours when *Ummat an-Nabī* sleeps, their souls ascend to make *sajda* at the Throne of Allāh. In that *sajda,* the soul is free to make remembrance of Allāh in the Divine Presence. That is why in Ṣalāt an-Najāt, that *sajda* is not here in *dunyā,* it is under the Holy Throne. *Awlīyāullāh* take their followers when they go in *sajda,* to the location in the Divine Presence at the Throne. Your heart must be well connected at that time, not to wander here and there; in this *sajda* you must be extremely careful with your thoughts, and you must be aware that you are in that Divine Presence! It is very heavy and that makes *awlīyā* shake, to consider how much you wasted your time in *dunyā*! Your *duʿā* there is accepted, so it is essential in that *sajda* to only make *duʿā* for your *Ākhirah,* not *dunyā.* But you may ask for *dunyā* also; ask what comes to the heart, such as:

> *Rabbanā ātinā fi 'd-dunyā ḥasanatan wa fi 'l-ākhirati ḥasanatan wa qinā ʿadhāba 'n-nār.*
>
> *Our Lord! Grant us good in this world and good in the Hereafter, and save us from the chastisement of the Fire.* (Sūrat al-Baqarah, 2:201)

When we prayed *Ṣalāt an-Najāt* behind Grandshaykh ʿAbdAllāh ق, we made *sajda* for one hour! Our foreheads, feet and hands become numb. We could not raise our heads (before Grandshaykh raised his). *Awlīyāullāh* know the importance of being in the Divine Presence, and as he was making *duʿā* and we were saying, *amīn.* The main difference is, his *duʿā* is not like our *duʿā,* because he is there under the Throne. That is not simple!

The Three Levels of Dhikr

The first level is *dhikrūllāh* is *bil-lisān, dhikr* by tongue, because the heart is not yet connected. This is considered "the Station of Heedlessness," because your heart is not able to open and that is called the *Maqām al-Awwam*, "the common people's station, *maqām* of *ghaflah*, heedlessness". Because with your tongue you can say, "*Allāh, Allāh*" and you are watching TV! How many of you are watching TV when doing *dhikr*? And that is also known as *dhikr ul-ʿada*, "the *dhikr* of habit." Like we make our prayers from habit, but it is not real worship. And we ask, "O Allāh! Change our *dhikr al-qalb* to real *dhikr*!"

The second level is to make *dhikr* by tongue and *dhikr* by heart. In the Naqshbandi Order, they train you to do *dhikr* by tongue and *dhikr* by heart, by assigning you to recite daily 2500 times *Allāh, Allāh* by tongue (verbally) and 2500 times *Allāh, Allāh* by heart (silently). As soon as you do that, you feel it. Take your beads or even without beads (*taṣbīḥ*); put your tongue on the roof of your mouth and you find your heart doing *dhikr, Allāh, Allāh*. That is *dhikru 'l-khawāṣ, "Dhikr* of the Chosen," assigned to some *murīds* by the shaykh. It is *dhikru 'l-ʿibādah, "dhikr* of (real) worship" and its fruit is *wa la-dhikrūllāhi akbar*, "Allāh will remember you in a Presence better than your presence."

Then the third level is, *dhikr al-khawāṣ al-khawāṣ, "Dhikr* of the Chosen of the Chosen," or *dhikr al-muḥabbatullāh, "Dhikr* of the Love of Allāh," in which all parts of body do *dhikr*. That is only for *awlīyāullāh*. When *dhikr* of the heart and tongue coincide, who does that *dhikr* is able to enter the Divine Presence, which is the best of *dhikr*, as Allāh ﷻ said:

> *Wadhkur rabbaka fī nafsika taḍaruʿan wa khufiyā wa dūn al-jahri min al-qawl wa lā takun mina 'l-ghāfilīn.*
>
> *And bring your Lord to remembrance in your (very) soul, with humility and in reverence, without loudness in words, in the mornings and evenings, and be not of those who are unheedful.* (Sūrat al-Aʿrāf, 7:205)

That means, don't make *dhikr* openly, but make it within yourself. Don't show that your beads are moving; that is "showing off," which is ego. One of Grandshaykh's representatives, Shaykh Ḥusayn ق, like Shaykh Nazim ق, I never saw him with beads in his hands during the day. He said, "We don't like to show off. Do *dhikr* at night, up to *Ishrāq*." They don't show they are carrying beads. Today they show five-hundred beads or even one-thousand beads, so long!

Tadaruʿan wa khīfatan wa dūn al-jahri min al-qawl, "Mention your Lord in yourself." Run to Him asking forgiveness, moving by your heart, afraid from losing His love to you, and inaudibly, without making a sound for people to see you are doing *dhikr*. Surrender and don't show off for others, with pride and arrogance.

Wa qawlahu ʿalayhis salām khayru 'dh-dhikr al-khafī.
The best of dhikr is the silent. (Ibn Hibbān)

Dhikr al-qalb sabaʿ diʿfan bi sabaʿ diʿf.
The dhikr of the heart is seventy times better.

When you multiply 2 x 2 it is 4, and 4 x 4 is 16, and the multiplication increases exponentially. So if you do 1000 *dhikr* of the heart, it is 70 times exponentially more than *dhikr* of the tongue. One-thousand times one-thousand is one-million, and then one-million times one-million is one-billion; that is two *dʿaf*. Three *daʿf* is one-billion times one-billion equals one-trillion. So see how high you go with 70 *daʿf*!

wa la-dhikrūllāhi akbar. This is a huge number; it has a limit, but you are happy with that huge number because Allāh's remembrance of you is without limits! Will He throw that one in the Hellfire? So say, *yā Allāh, yā Rabb*! If you mention "Allāh" one time, He will mention you and that is enough for your entire lifetime.

Wa 'dh-dhikr al-qalbi 'lladhī lā yasmaʿu al-ḥafaẓa ʿalā min dhikru 'l-lisān.
The dhikr of the heart is higher than the dhikr of the tongues which the angels hear. (Narrated by Ayesha in *Bayhaqī*)

SubhānAllāh, the knowledge never stops! May Allāh ﷻ forgive us and may Allāh ﷻ bless us.

Wa min Allāhi 't-tawfiq, bi ḥurmati 'l-ḥabīb, bi ḥurmati 'l-Fātiḥah.
And with Allāh is success. For the sake of the Beloved, for his sake we recite the opening chapter of Holy Qur'an.

Duties of Guides and Students

A'ūdhu billāhi min ash-Shayṭāni 'r-rajīm. Bismillāhi' r-Raḥmāni 'r-Raḥīm.
Nawaytu 'l-arbā'īn, nawaytu 'l-'itikāf, nawaytu'l-khalwah, nawaytu 'l-'uzlah,
nawaytu 'r-riyāḍa, nawaytu 's-sulūk, lillāhi Ta'alā fī hādhā 'l-masjid.
Atī'ūllāha wa atī'ū 'r-Rasūla wa ūli 'l-amri minkum. (4:59)

Mawlana Shaykh Nazim ق says that we have to ask *madad* from *awlīyāullāh* every time; it is proper *adab. Awlīyāullāh* ask their support from Prophet ﷺ, and so we ask support from Grandshaykh ق, from Mawlana Shaykh Nazim ق, and from every *walī* standing at the door of Prophet. They are our role models and the *murīd* tries to at stand their door to reach the Divine Presence. You cannot reach the Divine Presence without a teacher; they are there already. One of these *shuyukh aṭ-ṭā'ifa,* the shaykhs of *tazkīyyat an-nafs,* is Shaykh Shiblī ق. They are one group but they have different ways, because *awlīyā* are friends with each other and they know their limits.

Shaykh Shiblī said, "I mentioned You, not because I forgot You for the blink of an eye, but because it is easy on my tongue to refresh it and to say Your Name." That means he is speaking with his Lord. *Fa lammā wajadta annaka ḥādiran shahidta annaka mawjūd fī kulli makān,* "When I found that You are present, I testified that You are present in every place. I spoke to everyone without speech. I observed someone without looking through my eyes." They recite this poetry when they are in a trance-like state; then they cannot control themselves anymore and they are always trying to reveal what is in their hearts by expressing themselves.

Many people today remember their Lord when they are in an emotional state. Even if they are not *awlīyā,* when something horrible happens and they are sad, they feel like turning to their Lord and asking from Him, because it is there, but in normal life it is veiled with the darkness of this *dunyā.*

When someone you love dies and you are present there, you feel that majestic manifestation of al-Qahhār, (The Dominant), al-Jabbār (The Compeller), Qābiḍ (The Restricter), "the One in Whose Hand is everything." You feel these attributes and you begin to fear death, and maybe with that fear you cannot enter the deceased one's room as you feel uneasy. So you remember Allāh at that time. *Awlīyāullāh* are always in that state of feeling their return to Allāh. They are not like us; we like to live even longer than Sayyīdinā Nūḥ ﷺ!

One of the conditions of guiding to *dhikrūllāh* is, the *murshid* must be based in Islamic beliefs, *f'il-ʿaqāid wa fi'l-fiqh*, in beliefs and in jurisprudence, so that he can answer his followers' questions. If not, the *murīd* will begin to doubt his shaykh. This is one of the conditions of the shaykh of Ṭarīqat an-Naqshbandiyya as mentioned by Sayyīdinā Khālid al-Baghdādī ق. He must know *sharīʿatullāh*. If not, he must step down and surrender his status of shaykh to someone who knows it. Also, he must be able to perfect and discipline the hearts of followers to the highest level of perfection. He must know all kinds of *afāt an-nufūs*, the sicknesses of the self, and which sickness his *murīd* is in. He must also know the illnesses and how to cure the *murīds* from them. And not only will he guide them through their journey, but also if he found them in need for something, he has to provide it.

Sayyīdinā Khālid al-Baghdādī ق said, *Wa li-kulli min imkānahu la-atāhu min al-māl*, "The shaykh even has to give his *murīds* money to build them up, and he doesn't leave him without money." *Allāhu Akbar*! You can see how Mawlana Shaykh Nazim ق reacts to this. People come to his door for money. We used to say, "Why is Mawlana giving money to *murīds?*" He is not like us; he doesn't mind. He gives like an ocean! Allāh ﷻ gives to him and he gives.

Allāh ﷻ gave that *walī* power to see and observe all *ʿayb*, deficiencies, of his *murīd*. So from his perfection, he never exposes his *murīd;* he never says anything. Someone came complaining to me when I was in England and also by email, saying they have a problem with someone there who considers himself accomplished in everything and he is a senior one. He was begging me to tell Mawlana Shaykh Nazim ق. I said, "Okay, when I go to Cyprus. I cannot talk about these issues over the phone." I was entrusted with that matter, so when I went there I told Mawlana Shaykh Nazim ق. It was so simple. He said, "No, I never saw or heard that. I don't believe it. If it is true, let the person who is saying that come to me." He wants to cover and not expose. *Awlīyāullāh* hide their followers, they don't expose them or it might cause enmity. So they leave them and slowly, slowly fix them.

Someone told me here in America, in political events they keep the beast around them because if they let the beast loose, he might make too many problems. They keep petting the lion, not to let him loose. *Awlīyāullāh* pet us, and that is how they can catch us. Grandshaykh ق used to say, "I follow my *murīd* ninety-nine steps; I go according to what he or she likes.

When they are feeling they can trust me completely, I catch them. We go with them ninety-nine steps and then one step, they go with me."

Furthermore, the character of the shaykh must be rich in good manners and he must not be angry, except when you break Allāh's law. It is okay to get angry for Allāh's law, no problem. But for *dunyā* issues, the shaykh always forgives.

What is the duty of the *murshid* to his *murīd*? They are three. First, he has to put him on the right track to seek his journey. There are too many tracks, like a maze, and the *murīd* is not knowing where to begin or end. The *murshid* has to put him at the beginning of the maze. Second, he must inform the *murīd* when he has reached his goal; that is his duty. The *murīd* will be a guide for others and will be dressed with the Dress of Guidance. And third, the *murshid* will protect him when he is taking care of different followers around the world. The shaykh sends his senior *murīd* around the world to bring others to the shaykh.

And what are the duties of the *murīd* to his shaykh? First, he has to listen to whatever the shaykh says to him without question. Allāh said in Holy Qur'an:

Atiʿ ūllāh wa atiʿū 'r-Rasūl wa ūli 'l-amri minkum.
Obey Allāh, obey the Prophet, and obey those in authority among you.
(Sūrat an-Nisa, 4:59)

Here, "authority" means the shaykh. That is Allāh's order, and you cannot say no. You say, *samiʿna wa ataʿna,* "I hear and I obey." Can you do that? No, it is difficult. Even if you do it you still have doubts, thinking, "This doesn't work in my mind, it is not acceptable!" So he first has to listen to what the shaykh says. If the shaykh says "eat," then eat, "drink," then drink, "pray," then pray, "do this or don't do this." The second duty is, *kitmān sirr ash-shaykh.* If the *murīd* saw a secret of the shaykh, he must not expose it, even if it is something he doesn't like as he doesn't know the wisdom behind it.

Grandshaykh ق said, "One time I was in my seclusion under the order of Shaykh Sharafuddīn ق. During my seclusion he came to me." Your shaykh can come anytime during seclusion, but others cannot comer to you or it will interrupt the seclusion. He said, "'ʿAbdAllāh Effendi," meaning "respected ʿAbdAllāh," "Prepare yourself tomorrow. I will pass by you and take you somewhere." Grandshaykh ق was thinking, "O, I am coming out of seclusion to go somewhere." He had no doubt; his belief was straight forward, and he was that way since he was a boy. When he was young, he had to walk up a hill to reach his shaykh.

One day Shaykh Sharafuddīn ق was sitting with *ʿulamā* who said, "O Shaykh Sharafuddīn ق! You always give importance to that boy."

Shaykh Sharafuddīn ق said, "He is there at the bottom of the hill now. If I send someone to him saying, 'Your shaykh is telling you to go to Mecca,' then without coming to me to confirm, he will direct himself to Mecca and begin walking."

So now look at us and look at how strong his belief is, not like some people today who say they are representatives. Look at the belief. Can you tell someone now, "Close your store and take a one-month vacation." They will say, "How will I make my payments?"

Shaykh Sharafuddīn ق said, "Prepare yourself tomorrow, I am taking you."

No Questions in Tariqah

When Mawlana Shaykh Nazim ordered me into seclusion in 2005 in Damascus, he said, "Every Friday I want you to visit two *awlīyā,* Sayyīdinā Khālid al-Baghdādī ق and Sayyīdinā Muḥīyyidīn Ibn ʿArabī ق." I did my seclusion in Damascus, up on the mountain (in the home of Mawlana Shaykh Nazim on Jabal Qasiyoun). If the shaykh orders you to go out of seclusion, you do it; you go visit and come back. If you do that by their order it is alright, but you cannot do that on your own, or that breaks the seclusion.

Shaykh Sharafuddīn ق said, "Wait, I am coming." He came and took Grandshaykh ق to the big bazaar area in Istanbul, Kapalı Çarsa. It is a huge shopping area with a door at the beginning and a door at the end. You enter and you are inside, then they close the door in the evening and open it again in the morning. All kinds of people come there. When they reached the door, he said, "Let us hold each other's hand," and they stretched their arms. Although the door was bigger, but you could see that their hands were touching the door on both sides. Also, Allāh gave them above-average height, and everyone was able to pass under their arms.

Awlīyāullāh are not like us. Everyone coming in or going out had to go under their arms. Grandshaykh ق didn't ask Shaykh Sharafuddīn ق, "What is the wisdom?" There is no question in *ṭarīqah*. You do this, you don't change your mind. They stood all day until the noon prayer, then they prayed and came back. Time for *ʿAṣr* came, they prayed and came back. There are many mosques there and they went around. Then they stood there until the closing time, which was *Maghrib*, and then they left.

Shaykh Sharafuddīn ق was waiting to see if Grandshaykh ق will ask the wisdom. He didn't ask. That is his duty, *imtithāl al-amr,* to obey his order and *kitmān sirrih,* what he sees he has to hide (keep secret). He saw many things when people came and passed under their arms as it is an open, public place.

The next duty of *murīd* to *murshid* is *tʿaẓīm qadr ash-shaykh,* to raise higher the respect of the shaykh or his order. Some people might disrespect the shaykh if he orders them to go and open their hands at Kapali Çarşı (market) all day. They will say, "Why do I have to go there and raise my hand like that? People will say I am crazy and take me to the mental hospital." Grandshaykh ق kept quiet and did *tʿaẓīm amr ash-shaykh;* it is not to exalt, exaltation is for Allāh ﷻ; it is to elevate and honor whatever the shaykh does.

Grandshaykh ق never asked. At the end of the seclusion, Shaykh Sharafuddīn ق said, "ʿAbdAllāh Effendi! Do you know why I asked you to do that? I was ordered to hold these two doors so that anyone who passes will see us, and from seeing us, if Allāh likes, He will guide them to Islam," Because the light coming from *awlīyāullāh* can reach their hearts.

Grandshaykh ق said, "If a person looks at a *walī* with love, it means that *walī* is responsible for that person in *dunyā* and *in Ākhirah.* When someone loves you, it is because they feel that familiarity with you and light on you. That is how people feel with Mawlana Shaykh Nazim ق; they see his humility and love, and they are attracted. When people are attracted, then *awlīyāullāh* can work on their hearts.

So there are three things; obey the shaykh, keep his secret, and honor the respect given to him. That is one part. The second part for the *murīd* is: first, to have *adab* with Allāh; second, to have *adab* with Prophet, to respect and praise the Prophet ﷺ; and third, to have discipline with the shaykh and pious people. If you keep that, then you will reach the level of *dhikr* in the heart and you will be ready to be accepted. Then you are on the right track.

When a train comes, there are computers that put it on the right track. When pilots fly the plane, the computer guides the plane, even though the pilot might be sleeping. *Awlīyā's* hearts are responsible for their *murīds* and all of them are connected to his "auto pilot". Every *murīd's* wire is connected to the server of the shaykh.

But there is a question here. Sayyīdinā Muḥīyyidīn ibn ʿArabi ق wrote *Futūḥāt al-Makkīyah* (12 volumes). Western people and Muslims alike are drowning in what he wrote, and that was 1,000 years ago! Look how high he was. What about *awlīyāullāh* today? If they open those oceans, people will drown in them.

Yajib ʿalā shaykhun idhā ra'ā shaykhun ākhir, "It is an obligation of the shaykh that if he saw a shaykh higher than him in knowledge, to advise himself, and keep the service of the higher shaykh. This applies to him and his students. *Fa innahu ṣalāḥun wa ḥaqqihi wa ḥaqq aṣ-ḥābih,* "This will be righteousness and happiness for him and his followers." This means he is not cheating; he is not saying to his *murīds,* "I am the shaykh."

Those who consider themselves shaykhs, if they see another one higher, they have to drop their shaykh-hood and follow that shaykh who is higher, in order to reach happiness for him and his students. *Wa mattā lam yafʿal hadha laysa bi munṣafin li nafsihi wa ṣāḥbih,* "If he doesn't do that, he is not fair to himself. He is falling in a valley or well, and failed his *himmah,* what he was ordered."

In other words, if someone has a shaykh and he finds another shaykh who is higher, he has to follow him. If a *murīd* finds a *murīd* who is higher, he has to follow the one higher. If that senior *murīd* finds a senior *murīd* who is higher, he has to follow the one higher. If he doesn't do that, he is failing and he might be falling in love with the chair he is sitting on. *Ḥubban li 'r-riyāsah,* "in love with leadership," wanting that people follow him.

What was the character we mentioned in the beginning? He has to know all kinds of *fiqh* and all kinds of *ʿaqā'id.* If your belief is not correct, what is the benefit? You cannot say, "I am a Muslim," and you don't know what kind of faith you have.

The Prophet ﷺ said:

Walladhī nafsī bi-yadihi law an Mūsā kāna ḥayyan mā wasiʿahu illa an tabaʿnī.

By the One in Whose Hand is my soul, if Mūsā was alive in my time among you, he would have no choice but to follow me.

(Aḥmad, Abū Yaʿala, al-Bazzār)

So according to this *hadīth,* a shaykh must follow a shaykh that is higher than him. That is why Shaykh Ḥusayn Zakarīya in Ghana didn't take the Tijaniyya Ṭarīqah, which is spread throughout Ghana. Because at 14 years of age, he dreamt that a shaykh of the Naqshbandi Order gave him initiation. We sent someone to find him, who spent six months in Accra, but he could not find Shaykh Ḥusayn Zakarīya. When I landed, he was there at the airport waiting for me. Do you think he came there by himself? No! He had a dream in which Prophet ﷺ told him to go there and meet me. And that is how he got connected to the Naqshbandi Ṭarīqah. He was a shaykh, but he went to a higher shaykh. He has followers himself. Prophet said, "If Mūsā was alive in my time, he would have to follow me, and even Ilyas and ʿĪsā (would have to follow me)."

This also applies to the inheritors of the Prophet in this time; they must follow the one who is higher. That means you must take your followers to the right fountain. If not, it means you love leadership.

In Islam, there is a pyramid. Leadership is not accepted in Islam except in a hierarchy. You must go from down to up. You must show humbleness. The shaykh is showing humbleness. Who is showing humbleness now? These kings and presidents? They are not showing humbleness, they are stubborn, saying, "I am better!" Then what happens in the end, they fight each other. But if they sit together and say, "We have to work together and open the borders," at least the Muslim countries (would benefit). Now to visit those countries, they require a visa and a background check, and in those countries, they are blowing people up! If you want to go to Afghanistan, they have to check your background. Why? Go check the people living there!

Where did the current flood come in Pakistan? In Swat. What did they do there two months ago? They blew up the tomb of Data Ghanj Bakhsh, ʿAlī Hujwairi's ق *maqām. Awlīyāullāh* don't like that. Therefore, look what happened! They are punished. When punishment comes, it hits those who are good and those who are bad. So don't come against a *walīullāh,* living or dead. When they are dead, they are stronger, more powerful.

All prophets are under Sayyīdinā Muḥammad ﷺ. This must be an example for *shuyūkh* of *ṭarīqah;* all of them have to be under one. That is why you have to see who is under:

Wa fawqa kulli dhi ʿilmin ʿalīm.
Above every knower is a (higher) knower. (Sūrat Yūsuf, 12:76)

You have to find the highest *walī* and follow him or else you are not on the right way. This is important; it shows us principles of *ṭarīqah* and where we stand in regards to them. It is becoming a nice book for keeping discipline in *ṭarīqah,* which is important for all of us to learn. May Allāh bless this meeting and every meeting that calls people to Allāh ﷻ. May Allāh give long life to Mawlana Shaykh Nazim ق, and may all of us live to see Imām Mahdī ﷺ!

May Allāh ﷻ forgive us and may Allāh ﷻ bless us.

Wa min Allāhi 't-tawfiq, bi ḥurmati 'l-ḥabīb, bi ḥurmati 'l-Fātiḥah.
And with Allāh is success. For the sake of the Beloved, for his sake we recite the opening chapter of Holy Qur'an.

Types of Baya`, Their Conditions and Status

Aʿūdhu billāhi min ash-Shayṭāni 'r-rajīm. Bismillāhi' r-Raḥmāni 'r-Raḥīm. Nawaytu 'l-arbāʿīn, nawaytu 'l-ʿitikāf, nawaytu'l-khalwah, nawaytu 'l-ʿuzlah, nawaytu 'r-riyāḍa, nawaytu 's-sulūk, lillāhi Taʿalā fī hādhā 'l-masjid. Atīʿūllāha wa atīʿū 'r-Rasūla wa ūli 'l-amri minkum. (4:59)

Prophet ﷺ said, "If Mūsā was living, he would not be able except to follow me," because you have to follow the one higher than you. Also in Sharīʿah, you have to follow the one who is more knowledgeable than you. And also in *Ḥaqīqat*, you have to follow the one that Allāh ﷻ guided to the right path and whose knowledge is more than yours.

Imām ʿAbd al-Wahhāb ash-Shaʿrānī ق (d. Cairo 973 AH), one of the big scholars in Islam, said, *idhā rā'itu 'aḥadun aʿarafu minnī bi 't-tarīq lamadhtu ʿalayhi wa law kuntu maʿdhūnan min qabli li-shaykhin ākhir,* "If I see in my way, my journey, that journey never ends, and whatever you do is continuous and difficult. You have to face all these difficulties until you are able to reach the highest level of peacefulness and relaxation."

As it happened with Prophet Muḥammad ﷺ, he was tested and all his life was with obstacles, although he was the Seal of Messengers. Allāh ﷻ made him perfect, made him Insān al-Kāmil, "the Perfect Human Being." Allāh completed him, which means He is perfect and Allāh made him to reach perfection. When you reach perfection, it means you are not here; you are in the Divine Presence. The Divine Presence cannot accept anything except perfection. In *Ākhirah*, when Allāh ﷻ sends believers to *Jannah*, He makes believers reach perfection or else they cannot see Him in Paradise as Prophet said, "Allāh will be seen in Paradise." And that highest Paradise cannot allow anything except perfection.

There are lower levels of Paradise where there are all kinds of people who reached different levels, but the highest Paradise does not accept anyone except those who reach the highest level. The Prophet ﷺ reached perfection in *dunyā* when he was taken in *'Isrā wal-Miʿrāj* to *Qāba Qawsayni aw Adnā,* "within two bows' length". He reached the highest perfection while he was alive in *dunyā,* so he is the one that has to be followed. That is why *awlīyāullāh* say, "This journey is long and you cannot reach perfection."

Allāh ﷻ said:

Wa fawqa kulli dhī ʿilmin ʿalīm.
Above every knower is a (higher) knower. (Sūrat Yūsuf, 12:76)

It means there is something above everything; there is no limit, there is an infinite number of levels above and there is no limit to the levels of stations. As you move to one there is another, and another above that, so there are always higher levels. So for the Prophet, all his life there were difficulties and he said, *lā rāḥat fi 'd-dīn,* "There is no relaxation in religion." You have to keep struggling. He struggled until he reached perfection.

Idhā jā naṣrullāhi wal-fatḥ, wa ra'āit an-nāsa yadkhulūna fi dīni llāhi afwājā.
When Allāh's support comes you will see people entering the Path of Allāh in big numbers. (Sūrat an-Nasr, 110:1)

So Allāh ﷻ gave Prophet ﷺ that *nasr,* victory, He also made the inheritors of Prophet ﷺ capable of giving victory to their followers, to enter into their *ḥaẓīra,* garden. They will enter inside their garden to be taken care of and to be safe, and they will be guided to that road to reach the presence of Prophet!

That is why Shaykh ʿAbd al-Wahhāb ash-Shaʿrānī ق said, *idhā rā'itu aḥadun aʿarafu minnī bi 'ṭ-ṭarīq lamadhtu ʿalayhi wa law kuntu mā'dhūnan min qabl li-shaykhin ākhir.* "If I find someone more knowledgeable than me in the path, I will become his student." So don't say, "No, I don't want to be a student." You always follow and listen to someone who knows more than you; go and sit in his association. Don't say, "I have no permission." No, especially if someone is in the same order you are, listen to each other and don't argue; you might get wisdom.

He said, "Even if I am given authority to conduct teachings or lead *dhikrūllāh* and I find someone in that *ṭarīqah* who knows more than I do, I will listen to what he says. Even if there is one *mā'dhūn* in the east and one in the west, and one in the north and one in the south, one should go and listen to the one with more knowledge. Don't say, 'I am the shaykh.' No, you are not the shaykh. That is why I went to listen to one shaykh after another."

Levels have no limits at which the servant will stop; there is always ascension, so go to the higher level. *Alḥamdulillāh* that Allāh ﷻ guided us to the highest! But when you are in an association and you are not in the presence of Sulṭān al-Awlīyā, if there is another *mā'dhūn* who is higher than you, go and listen and learn. Not everything has been given to you. So try to humble yourself. *fa idhan luzūm khidmat ash-shaykh al-akmal minhu.* "It is obligatory for a shaykh who knows himself to be lower than the other shaykh to sit and listen to that shaykh." As it is mentioned and happened in Holy Qur'an. Today they say, "Where is it?" They are authorized to give lectures and lead *dhikr,* and they think they are so high that they prevent those who follow them from listening to someone else. That is a sickness in them. They tell them, "That one doesn't know anything and we know everything!" If that is the case, why did Allāh ﷻ send Sayyīdinā Mūsā to Sayyīdinā Khiḍr? Mūsā was at a higher level than him, but there was a knowledge given to Khiḍr that Sayyīdinā Mūsā did not have. Allāh ﷻ told him, "Go and seek him in a journey." So he went with his servant to seek him in that journey

With everyone there is a taste that the other doesn't carry, and that is the case with Sayyīdinā Khiḍr ؑ and Sayyīdinā Mūsā ؑ. So that is a sign to us, that if we are not near our perfect teacher, Sulṭān al-Awlīyā Mawlana Shaykh Nazim al-Haqqani ق, if there is someone of higher level than us coming to our area, he will be the one to conduct the ṣuḥbah and we will go and listen to him. But today the apples and oranges are together in one basket, so what can you do? The one who doesn't humble himself and listen to those higher than him will never smell the smell of *ṭarīqah,* because refused to go to a higher paradise. That is because one paradise leads to another. You sit in one paradise and that opens to the second, then the second opens to the third, and so on. You cannot open from the first to the fourth, it is impossible.

Today even children know more than us, with children's video games. Sometimes I see children playing them, especially in Cyprus, not here. They are playing these games in which you finish one part successfully and it opens to another level, and it goes like a gate, and you move through it to open another level. It is as if the people who made these games, *subhānAllāh,* were inspired in their hearts! You don't jump from one level to a higher level; no, you go in a sequence and you have to go through all the levels. So the one who tries to jump through levels will stay in the first level and never reach his destiny, his goal.

Awlīyāullāh in previous times never gave *baya*ʿ before the student reached a certain level. It was not like today, when the *baya*ʿ is being spread quickly by Mawlana Shaykh, in his wisdom, since time is short and ignorance is filling *dunyā.* But in the past, the seeker had to reach a certain level before the shaykh would give *baya*ʿ, and only after he had a dream or vision of Prophet authorizing him to give *baya*ʿ to that one. *Baya*ʿ was extremely difficult to get. As I said many times, Grandshaykh ق never gave *baya*ʿ to anyone. We know of only two that have *baya*ʿ, and of all those who came to him he never gave his hand and recited *Āyat al-Baya*ʿ, the Verse of Initiation. They used to sit with him and say, "You are our shaykh."

Previously they used to give *baya*ʿ in the way of the narration of Sayyīdinā ʿUmar ﷺ, where Jibrīl came in the form of a man wearing very shining white clothes, which was impossible in that area and time, since it was dust and desert, but he didn't have any sign of travel. He entered the form of a man and sat on his knees with the Prophet ﷺ sitting in front of him on his knees, and their knees were touching and their hands were on their thighs. So in *ṭarīqah*, the way of dissemination or transmission of *baya*ʿ has to be in such way, as Sayyīdinā Jibrīl ﷺ was in the presence of Prophet ﷺ, putting his hands on his thighs. Then the shaykh has to make association with and receive authority from Prophet in the night, in *istikhāra*.

And the Prophet ﷺ said:

Mā khāba man istikhār wa lā nadm man istashār.

No one failed who made the guidance prayer, and no one regretted who consults.

That answer comes from a high level. And one incident, the only incident we know that happened in this way, was with Shaykh al-Lasūni ق in Istanbul, when Mawlana Shaykh ق was young and went to him to follow and take *baya*ʿ. He said, "O my son, your *amānat* is not with me." He didn't quickly give him *baya*ʿ to "win" one more follower; they knew their limits. He said, "Your *amānat* is with someone in Damascus. Go and find him, Shaykh ʿAbdAllāh al-Faʾiz ad-Daghestani."

How did he know? They had no relationship. There was a world war, a big war, and to make a long story short, Mawlana Shaykh went moving from one place to another, one place to another, to go to Damascus to take *baya*ʿ from Grandshaykh ق.

This was narrated by Grandshaykh. Mawlana Shaykh Nazim passed through Aleppo, Hama, and Homs. The war was very fierce where the French and English were fighting each other inside Damascus. And Mawlana landed in Homs and stayed one year in Khalid ibn Walīd's *maqām*; he is buried there. Mawlana Shaykh was not going out, he was studying

Sharī'ah. It was like *khalwah* in one room. Then slowly he was moving to Damascus, but he didn't know where to go. He ended up in a place called Mīdān, which still exists, and he asked people there, "Does anyone know a Daghestani shaykh?"

They said, "Yes, there."

Why did he go to that area, not to Marja for example, or to Rukn ad-Dīn or Romana? Because Allāh ﷻ guided him. He reached the door of that house and Grandshaykh ق opened the door and said, "Come."

He said, "*Sayyīdī*, I am on my way and they sent me to you. I am on the way for *Hijra* to *Madīnatu 'l-Munawarra*."

Grandshaykh said, "Stay here tonight and I will make *istikhāra*."

That is the formal way, *mā khāba man istikhār*, and you will not be disappointed if you make a request to see Prophet in a dream. So he said, "You rest and spend the night, I will make you food." And they didn't talk more. The next morning after *Fajr* he said to him, "*Yā waladī*! There is no permission to go to *Madīnatu 'l-Munawarra*. There is more need for you to be in your country." And he sat as Sayyīdinā Jibrīl عليه السلام did with Prophet ﷺ and he gave Mawlana Shaykh *baya'* and sent him to where there was war, back to Cyprus. Mawlana didn't say, "No." It was his first time meeting the shaykh and he gave Mawlana the order to go back. Look at how much belief he had, when he had that intention, and he was counting the days until he would go to *Madīnatu 'l-Munawarra* and be *mujāwar*, the neighbor of Prophet! It was as if Grandshaykh blew up all his expectations.

To Leave Your Expectations

But Grandshaykh ق was teaching him, "No, it is not according to your expectations, but according to our decision." People might expect a lot, but *awlīyāullāh* will change it for you and cut it down. And then the shaykh passes that *baya'* to that *murīd* one-to-one, and passes to him what he needs to know from *ṭarīqah*. And then after he is sitting, he takes the right hand of the *murīd* as if shaking hands. After that, they both recite *istighfār*, then recite *Āyat al-Baya'*:

Innal-ladhīna yubai'ūnak innamā yubai'yūnallāh. yadullāhi fawqa aydīyhim faman nakatha fa innamā yankuthu 'alā nafsihi wa man awfā bimā 'ahada 'alayhullāh fa-sayu'tīyhi ajran 'azīmā.

Behold, all who pledge their allegiance to you pledge their allegiance to God: the hand of God is over their hands. Hence, he who breaks his oath breaks it only to his own hurt, whereas he who remains true to what he has pledged unto God, on him will He bestow a reward supreme. (Sūrat al-Fatḥ, 48:10)

Then they close their physical eyes, and by the power of the shaykh the eyes of the heart will open. That is real *baya*ʿ! All of them are real with Mawlana's *barakah,* but that is the formal, strong *baya*ʿ. As soon as they close their eyes, by the power of Prophet ﷺ, the shaykh opens the eyes of the *murīd's* heart. Then when he opens his eyes, he will see himself in a different level. That cannot be described; you feel goose bumps and your whole body is numb, receiving. You are able then, at that moment, to begin *dhikrūllāh bi ʿIsm adh-Dhāt.*

The shaykh will make *talqīn* as you make *talqīn* at the grave of the one who just passed, saying, *yā ʿAbdAllāh qul ash-hadu an lā ilāha illa-Llāh...* the tradition of reminding the deceased to recite Kalīmat ash-Shahadah. Today they throw the body in the grave and run for the inheritance, and those who came to be with the family run to eat the food served on behalf of the deceased! The loved ones give them food, since they came to the graveyard, and everyone is running to eat rice and meat (no *adab*)!

So that *talqīn ʿIsm adh-Dhāt,* which encompasses all the Names of Allāh, passes from the shaykh's tongue and heart to the *murīd's* tongue and heart; I am speaking here of the Naqshbandi Order. Then the shaykh will give *talqīn* on the heart of the *murīd* as if he is in the Divine Presence, visualizing what he was not able to see before. He is seeing something he was not able to see, and his heart is pumping and trembling, and he will say *ʿIsmullāh.* He says, *Allāh Hūuuuuuuu, Allāh Hūuuuuuuu, Allāh Hūuuuuuuu Ḥaqq,* three times. What the *murīd* receives from hidden treasures in these moments is only for him or her, and the *murīd* has no right to mention or disclose what the shaykh opens to his heart, and this will be a secret.

So that gives us an idea of the difference between what we understand of *baya*ʿ and what is the reality of *baya*ʿ. And you can compare now which one is stronger: what we are receiving today or what they were receiving before? Which is stronger? In reality, what you are receiving today is higher, but you cannot see it. It will be given without your knowledge. Before it will be given and you can know it, your body will know what it has been given and you can feel it daily, that contentment, and the level in which you have been put, and the level from which you are ascending.

You are not given that *baya*ʿ unless you went into the journey, and you have reached the level of *muḥibīn*, lovers, having passed through *Darajāt al-*

Mubtadi'īn, "Rank of the Initiates"; and *Darajāt al-Musta'id,* "Rank of the Prepared;" and then you reach *Darajāt al-Murīdīn,* "Rank of the *Murīds.*"

So the *murīd* in Naqshbandi Ṭarīqah is like a shaykh; he is not given until he is like a mountain, then he is given *baya'*. In previous times you went to these three levels and then you became a *murīd,* then they gave you *baya'*. Today they give the *baya'* since there is too much ignorance. You are not allowed to see it, as children are not given diamonds since they don't know their value and cannot be trusted to protect them.

Awlīyāullāh say, "There is the box and we will keep it for you." But in previous times they gave you the box and you saw it, since you had already passed through the three levels. Today, if we stay in the level of *muḥibīn,* that is a great job you did. So the shaykh is giving *'Ism adh-Dhāt* on the follower's heart by saying, *"Allāh Hūuu, Hūuu Allāh."* It means from the Beautiful Name "Allāh," you have to go further into the Absolute Unknown of the Reality of the Essence, as mentioned in Sūrat al-Ikhlāṣ, *Qul Hūwa,* "Say, the Unknown, that is Allāh!"

As a *murīd* you begin with the opposite; you begin with "Allāh," because Allāh ﷻ can be described by Ninety-nine Beautiful Names and Attributes: *Allāh, ar-Raḥmān, al-Quddūs, as-Salām,* and so on. Allāh ﷻ leads you through the Ninety-nine Beautiful Names so you can reach the reality that you will never know about, and it is in Allāh's Hands, Allāh's treasures.

"Say, *Yā* Muḥammad! The One Who cannot be known is 'Allāh'!" So we begin with Allāh, then *Huuuuu;* we don't begin with *Huuuuu.* In Holy Qur'an you begin with *Huuuuu,* then Allāh. So he will give you that and you will see the Divine Attributes and visions of the Divine Presence in different colors. You will make *istighfār* and read Ikhlāṣ and you will be put in the *silsilah,* the chain and *rābiṭah* of your shaykh and you will be connected in that chain.

You will not do that until you are sure. You cannot give *baya'* and then one day you are strong and one day you are weak, as Allāh ﷻ says in Holy Qur'an"

Thumma āmanū, thumma kafarū, Inna alladhīna āmanū thumma kafarū thumma āmanū thumma kafarū thumma izdādū kufran lam yakūnillāhu li-yaghfir' lahum walā li-yahdiyahum sabīl.

Lo! Those who believe, then disbelieve and then (again) believe, then disbelieve, and then increase in disbelief, Allāh will never pardon them, nor will He guide them unto a way. (Sūrat an-Nisa, 4:137)

So that is why they don't give the strong *baya*ʿ today; that cannot happen until it is known that you will not change, until you know that your shaykh *yunaba'u* ʿ*anhu fī tarbīyyat al-khalq,* represents the knowledge given to him from the heart of Prophet, in order to raise up his *murīds* and those who come for guidance. So Prophet ﷺ said, "Mention that Allāh ﷻ is the cure for hearts." (Daylami in *Musnad al-Firdaws*.) All that is by being connected to *Insān al-Kamil,* the Perfect Human Being, Prophet ﷺ! We will continue next time with that.

So the *baya*ʿ before has its own taste and with it you feel able to know things that you never knew, because the body is allowed to see what the soul is seeing. They give you a password for that, and allow your access, and you are a seeker in that journey. But today the *baya*ʿ is general and you are given more, but you are not allowed to see it as it is too much darkness all around. Before it was less and today is higher and that depends on the power of the shaykh. So try to reach the real *baya*ʿ, then you will experience the taste of real fruit, not only see the fruit but to taste them! That is what is the end-goal for *awlīyā* on their followers, a tasty garden, that you move from one to another and taste the honey and the fruits.

May Allāh ﷻ forgive us and may Allāh ﷻ bless us.

Wa min Allāhi ʿ*t-tawfiq, bi ḥurmati* ʿ*l-ḥabīb, bi ḥurmati* ʿ*l-Fātiḥah.*
And with Allāh is success. For the sake of the Beloved, for his sake we recite the opening chapter of Holy Qur'an.

The Status of Dhikrullah in Holy Qur'an and Tariqah

Aʿūdhu billāhi min ash-Shayṭāni 'r-rajīm. Bismillāhi' r-Raḥmāni 'r-Raḥīm.
Nawaytu 'l-arbāʿīn, nawaytu 'l-ʿitikāf, nawaytu'l-khalwah, nawaytu 'l-ʿuzlah,
nawaytu 'r-riyāḍa, nawaytu 's-sulūk, lillāhi Taʿalā fī hādhā 'l-masjid.
Atīʿūllāha wa atīʿū 'r-Rasūla wa ūli 'l-amri minkum. (4:59)

We must ask support from *awlīyāullāh,* who in turn ask support from Prophet ﷺ. And we say, *Atiʿ ūllāh wa atiʿū 'r-Rasūl wa ūli 'l-amri minkum.* "Obey Allāh, obey the Prophet, and obey those in authority among you." (4:59)

Aʿūdhu billāhi min ash-Shayṭān ir-rajīm. Bismillāhi' r-Raḥmāni 'r-Raḥīm. We consider the recitation of, *Aʿūdhu billāhi min ash-Shayṭān ir-rajīm* is *dhikrūllāh.* When we say that, Shayṭān will be chained and stopped. And then we say *Bismillāhi' r-Raḥmāni 'r-Raḥīm.* By reciting this, you enter that garden of Allāh, Who created everything and made it appear by *Bismillāhi' r-Raḥmāni 'r-Raḥīm.* As He said, in the verse to Prophet:

> *Iqrā bismi rabbik alladhī khalaq.*
> *Read in the Name of your Lord, Who created.* (Sūrat al-Alaq, 96:1)

Creation has been given to Prophet and that is in the first revelation, "Read!" Prophet ﷺ said, "What am I going to read?" "Read in the name of Your Lord." *Bismillāhi' r-Raḥmāni 'r-Raḥīm* is the key to Paradise and the key to everything. Any *ʿamal* that doesn't begin with *bismillāh* is cut, *maqtuʿa;* it has leaks in its pipe and no water will come to its end. Therefore, when we dress we say *bismillāh,* when we eat we say *bismillāh,* when we drink, when we go out, when we do any work, we say *bismillāh.* That is the key to success. *Awlīyāullāh* know that *Bismillāhi' r-Raḥmāni 'r-Raḥīm* is *dhikrūllāh,* so they keep in their hearts remembrance of their Lord and are always doing *dhikrūllāh* in their hearts.

Prophet ﷺ said:

> *The remembrance of the prophets is considered worship, while the remembrance of the pious is expiation (of sins), and the remembrance of death is charity.*

And the remembrance of pious people—for example, you or anyone who remembers Allāh is considered pious—*kafāratun,* takes away sins. Prophets have no sins to take away, so *dhikr* for them is worship, and for pious ones it is a cleansing or waiving of sins.

The Prophet ﷺ said (continuing the *hadīth*):

Wa dhikr al-mawtu ṣadaqatun.
To remember death is charity.

When you make *dhikr* with the intention of remembering your death, it will be considered *ṣadaqah,* like when you give a donation in the Way of Allāh. It will be written for you from beginning to end as if you are giving *ṣadaqah,* that you paid the *zakāt* of your entire life! That remembrance of death will protect you on the Day of Resurrection.

Wa dhikru 'l-qabr yuqarribukum mina 'l-jannah.
And when you remember the grave, that will take you nearer to Paradise.

What is after the grave? It is either Paradise or punishment. So if you remember you are leaving *dunyā,* you are giving *ṣadaqah* and to remember your grave makes you near Paradise.

As Prophet ﷺ said:

Those who are pious, Allāh will free their souls and turn their graves into a piece of Paradise. (Ad-Daylami in *Musnad al-Firdaws*)

Dhikr is better than ṣadaqah. (Abū Shuʿayb in *Musnad al-Thawab*)

In Ramadan, people run to give *ṣadaqah,* but after Ramadan they stop, as if there is nothing left, all engines are down. Your donation is limited, or you do it only one time. That is why *awlīyā* say put a box in your house and when you go in or out always put *ṣadaqah,* to keep it running. The same is with your *dhikr,* keep it running; then it is considered *ṣadaqah,* whether you are walking, standing, or moving. In every moment, you are doing *dhikrūllāh.*

There are many *aḥadīth* and verses of Holy Qur'an mentioning *dhikrūllāh.*

Adh-dhikr al-ladhī la yasmaʿu al-ḥafaẓa khayrun min dhikr al-ladhī yasmaʿ al-ḥafaẓa bi sabaʿīn daʿf.
The (silent) dhikr the angels do not hear is better than the (loud) dhikr heard by angels by seventy times.

So *dhikr khafī*, (silent *dhikr*) by the heart, is seventy times better than the loud *dhikr*.

Allāh ﷻ said:

Yā ayyuhalladhīna āmanū 'dhkurullāha dhikran kathīra.
O you who believe! Celebrate the praises of Allāh, and do this often.
(Sūrat al-'Aḥzāb, 33:41)

Fadhkurullāha ʿinda 'l-mashʿari 'l-ḥarām.
Celebrate the praises of Allāh at the sacred monument.
(Sūrat al-Baqarah, 2:198)

Wadhkurūḥu kamā hadākum.
And celebrate His praises as He has directed you. (Sūrat al-Baqarah, 2:198)

Al-ladhīna yadhkurūna Allāh qiyāman wa quʿūdan wa ʿalā junūbīhim.
Men who celebrate the praises of Allāh, standing, sitting, and lying down on their sides. (Sūrat 'Āli ʿImrān, 3:191)

Fa idhā qadaytum manāsikakum fadhkurūllāh ka-dhikrikum ābaūkum aw ashadda dhikrā.
So when you have accomplished your holy rites, celebrate the praises of Allāh.
(Sūrat al-Baqarah, 2:200)

Wadhkur rabbaka fī nafsika taḍaruʿan wa khufiyā wa dūn al-jahri min al-qawl wa lā takun mina 'l-ghāfilīn.
And bring your Lord to remembrance in your (very) soul, with humility and in reverence, without loudness in words, in the mornings and evenings, and be not of those who are unheedful. (Sūrat al-Aʿrāf, 7:205)

Wa la-dhikrullāhi akbar.
And remembrance of Allāh is the greatest (thing in life).
(Sūrat al-ʿAnkabūt, 29:45)

There are many verses in the Holy Qur'an about *dhikrūllāh* that show its importance. Just as the heart is mentioned approximately one-hundred times by name in Holy Qur'an, *dhikrūllāh* is mentioned many places as well, as it is the work of the heart. So keep *dhikrūllāh* on your tongue and you will be safe in this life and the Next Life.

Al-Fuḍayl ق said, "It has reached us that Allāh says, 'O My servant, remember Me one hour after *Fajr*.'" This is the saying of *awlīyā* and is why they keep *dhikrūllāh* for one hour after *Fajr*, as mentioned by Fuḍayl ق, who also said, "And after *ʿAṣr* prayer, remember Allāh for one hour." That is why if you want to follow this path, they will tell you, "Be sure to keep one hour after *Fajr* and one hour after *ʿAṣr*. Then that is enough for you to guarantee what is between them, that you will be safe." Those who cannot do that, as time now is changing, *awlīyāullāh* might reduce that to five minutes. So don't run away, sit and do five minutes after *ʿAṣr* time and five minutes after *Fajr*. Don't be lazy like us, and he is always sitting and doing *dhikrūllāh*.

Wa qāla ghanīmatuh majālis adh-dhikru al-jannah.
And he said, "What you gain from associations of dhikrūllāh by yourself or with people is Paradise for sure." (Aḥmad, at-Ṭabarānī)

If you want Paradise in *dunyā* and *Ākhirah,* make *dhikrūllāh*. All of *taṣawwuf* is not only moral excellence, which doesn't come free; it works after your heart is pumping with *dhikrūllāh*. So what makes your heart in the Divine Presence will make you *yartāh fil al-jinān*, grazing and roaming in Paradise. In *dunyā,* you will always be in that *tajallī* of Paradise when you remember Allāh ﷻ.

The Prophet ﷺ said:

Law anna rajulayn aqbala āḥadahumā min as-sūq fī hijrihi danānīr yuʿtīhā, wa'l-ākhir yadhkurallāh kāna dhākirullāhi afḍal.
If there were two men, one a man with money in his lap and he is passing it to people, and there was one who is sitting remembering Allāh, that one who is remembering Allāh is better than the one distributing money.

This is to encourage remembrance. *Taṣawwuf* is based on *dhikrūllāh*. If there is no *dhikr,* there is no *taṣawwuf.* Moral excellence comes with good behavior by remembering Allāh in different ways through his Beautiful Names and Attributes. When you remember Allāh by His Ninety-nine

Names, the *tajallī* of these Beautiful Names takes you over. The *tajallī* will make you feel Goosebumps from the presence of angels that bring those Beautiful Names to dress you. That is what takes you from bad manners to good manners; without you trying to avoid the bad manners, it will carry and throw you to the good side!

To Remove Yourself from Dunya

This just came to me now, so I will share it. When I was young, I was ordered by Grandshaykh ق to put a cover when doing *dhikr*. He ordered me not to be open as we are here. It means to tighten your space or don't have huge space. Similarly, when doing seclusion, we do it in closed small spaces. In 1997, I was asked by Mawlana Shaykh Nazim ق to do seclusion in Istanbul. I went to that *masjid* and on the roof they had built a grave the size of this *minbar*, perhaps six feet long by four feet wide. When you sit in that, you have to bend down.

When I phoned Mawlana Shaykh Nazim ق, he said, "Where did they tell you to stay?"

I said, "They put me in a grave they built on the roof."

He said, "What will you do?"

I said, "I am going to enter it."

He was checking me. And that grave was scary; they close it when you go in and only let you out to do *wuḍū*. Then with Mawlana's mercy, he said, "You passed the test. Go and take a room." But in reality, years before, seclusion used to be done in a cemetery. You would sit in a closed grave between the deceased and listen to what goes on at night from different graves! It was not so easy. That is why you have to cover yourself. If you cover yourself you will know what we mean. If you want real *baya'*, cover yourself, then you will be visualizing or seeing what cannot be seen at that moment.

So I was 22 years of age then, covering myself during *dhikr* and reciting, *"Lā ilāha illa-Llāh, lā ilāha illa-Llāh, lā ilāha illa-Llāh."* Naqshbandis recite *"Allāh, Allāh,"* but the *adab* is to recite, *"Lā ilāha illa-Llāh"* and then recite *'Ism adh-Dhāt* (Name of the Holy Essence), which is *"Allāh, Allāh."*

I was reciting loudly in a melodious voice. At that moment I began to feel something unusual and I was afraid. I was shaking and wanted to take the cover off, because it became heavy and difficult. As what happened today in *Fajr*, the first *raka'at* was silent because they didn't let me to say it out loud, it was not coming, but I was hearing Shaykh Sahib saying *"Allāhu Akbar, Allāhu Akbar,"* and then the second *raka'at* was in a loud voice. That is why I made *Sajdat as-Sahūw* at the end.

So, I felt like I could not take it anymore and at that moment the presence of Prophet ﷺ came and entered from my head. As Prophet was entering slowly, slowly, I was shaking, but I felt the beauty of that presence, which overtook me completely. Then at that moment, what happened, happened. This is what I wanted to say, that when you cover yourself and do *dhikrūllāh,* cutting yourself entirely from *dunyā,* then *awlīyāullāh* and Prophet's ﷺ presence will reach you. That was Allāh's, Prophet's, and our shaykh's favor, that Prophet overtook my body completely and I was feeling myself enveloped in that beauty for many, many days after that.

Thus, if you disconnect yourself from *dunyā,* you will be able to take away your bad characters. Every Beautiful Name has its taste and remedy to cure you of your bad behaviors and forbiddens. There are 800 forbiddens that *awlīyā* count and their only remedy is *dhikrūllāh.* That is why every Friday, Thursday, or Saturday, you do *dhikr* with different Beautiful Names, because Āhlu 'l-Ṭarīqah do that and we do like them. The highest Name that is above all Beautiful Names and Attributes, *'Ismullāh al-jami'ī lil-'Asmā wa'ṣ-Ṣiffāt,* is "Allāh," it encompasses all Names and Attributes.

That is why on behalf of their followers, the shaykh of this *ṭāi'fa,* group, assigns them an *awrād* of reciting *Allāh, Allāh, Allāh, Allāh,* to clean them through their recitation of the Beautiful Names and Attributes and send them to that ocean of the Name "Allāh.". Some assign it for recitation 5,000 times a day and some 10,000 times. If you are a beginner in that Way, then it is 1,500 times a day. *Allāhumā ṣalli 'alā Sayyīdinā Muḥammad* ﷺ!

Illa an yashā Allāhu wa 'dhkur rabbaka idhā nasīta wa qul 'asā an yahdīyanī rabbī li aqraba min hādhā rashada.
Except (with the saying), "If Allāh wills!" And remember your Lord when you forget and say, "It may be that my Lord guides me to a nearer way of truth than this." (Sūrat al-Kahf, 18:24)

Itba' as-sayīāt al-ḥasanat tamḥūhā.
Follow the bad deed with a good deed, as it erases it. (Tirmidhī)

When you commit a sin, immediately follow it with *"astaghfirullāh;"* that will erase the sin. Don't say, "I have too many sins," no, don't complain or it will be as if you are contradicting the verse of Holy Qur'an:

Wadhkur rabbaka idhā nasīta.
Remember Allāh when you forget. (Sūrat al-Kahf, 18:24)

When you commit a sin, follow it with goodness and that will erase it. We know when we do something wrong, then we say *astaghfirullāh'* that will erase everything.

Wa qāla man aḥaba liqā-allāh aḥab Allāhu liqāuh wa man kariha liqāuh karihallāhu liqāuh.
Who likes to meet Allāh, Allāh loves to meet him, and who hates to meet Allāh, Allāh hates to meet him. (Muslim, Aḥmad and Tirmidhī)

Man āt'a'Allāh faqad dhakr-Allāh wa in qallat ṣalātahu wa sīyāmahu wa tilāwata 'l-qur'an. wa man 'asa 'Llāh faqad nasīy 'Llāh wa in kathurat ṣalātuhu wa ṣīyāmahu wa tilāwata 'l-qur'ān.
Whoever obeys Allāh remembers Allāh, even if he doesn't do extra prayers and extra fasting, and doesn't read Qur'an (and whoever disobeys Allāh has forgotten Allāh, even if he does much prayer and fasting and reading of Qur'an). (Bayhaqi, ibn Mundhir, Sa'īd ibn Mansūr, Ṭabarānī)

It means when you obey Allāh, you remember Him, and when you remember Him, you obey Him.

Lā yaqu'd qawmun yadhkurūn Allāha Ta'alā illa ḥafathum al-malā'ikata wa ghashīyahum ar-raḥmata wa nazalat 'alayhim as-sakīnata wa dhakarahumullāha fīman 'indah.
Never do a group of people sit in circles remembering Allāh except that the angels will surround them and they will be covered with mercy and tranquility descends on them, and Allāh remembers them to those in His Presence. (Muslim)

When you go to a meeting with a king, you wear a nice dress with medallion from the king. Then the next day when you come to door, you are admitted immediately as you already have the medallion from the king.

Likewise, can anyone stop you from entering Paradise when you come dressed with *dhikrūllāh?* Saying *lā ilāha illa-Llāh* one time will dress you with that mercy and you will be admitted to Paradise!

For example, military personnel have on their uniforms rows of ribbons that distinguish what they achieve, so the military people know them. On the Day of Judgment the believers will come with all these ornaments and the doors of Paradise will open for them. Depending on what ornaments you have, different doors will be opened to you. May Allāh give us high levels in Paradise! Don't follow those people whose hearts are heedless.

> *Waṣbir nafsak maʿ alladhīna yadaʿūna rabbahum bil-ghadāti wa 'l-ʿashīyya yurīdūna wajhahu wa lā taʿdaw ʿaynayka ʿanhum turīdu zīnat al-ḥayāt ad-dunyā wa lā tutʿi man aghfalnā qalbahu ʿan dhikrinā wa't-tabaʿ hawāhu wa kāna amruhu furuṭā.*
> *And keep your soul content with those who call on their Lord morning and evening seeking His Face, and let not your eyes pass beyond them seeking the pomp and glitter of this life, nor obey any whose heart We have permitted to neglect the remembrance of Us, one who follows his own desires, whose case has gone beyond all bounds.* (Sūrat al-Kahf, 18:28)

Stay with those whose hearts are in remembrance day and night. Those who are doing *dhikrullāh* are more important than anyone else. That is why you cannot leave weekly *dhikrūllāh* except for three circumstances: you are traveling, you have a guest, or you are sick. Don't leave it; you may even do it at home, with or without company. *Dhikrūllāh* is the most honored worship. It is the best, the greatest, and the most complete, perfect form of the aspect of purifying and cleaning the hearts.

So if you want to purify the heart from the sickness of *dunyā,* stay on *dhikrūllāh.* And it is not only to clean and purify the heart, but to sweeten it as well. It is as if you put sugar in tea, coffee, and juice. If you don't put sugar, it will not be sweet. It is said that if worshipers, *ʿabidīn*, spend their day and night in all kinds of worship, rarely will they get a purified heart. That is why you see scholars are arrogant, because they feel that they are different, and higher than others. *Awlīyāullāh* say that even if they are worshipping day and night, *qalama taḥṣala taṣfiyya qulūbihim*, rarely will they achieve to sift something. "Sifting" hearts keeps the good in the heart and removes the bad.

And those who remember Allāh ﷻ, when they finish their prayers and *ʿibadāt,* they are busy with *dhikrūllāh,* and they don't say, "Pray your prayer and then wear your jeans and go to the mall," as today some famous *imāms* say. Also, *fa amma adh-dhākirūn lamā yashtaghil bi dhikrillāh ʿalā ad-dawām lā yashudhu minhum aḥad illa ḥaṣal ʿala ḥaqīqatih,* "Those who remember Allāh all the time, will be dressed with lots of secrets and the connection to the Divine Presence," because *dhikrūllāh* is the only *ʿamal* the heart can do that contains all the different principles of remembering Allāh.

It will bring you nearer and nearer to *Maqām al-Yaqīn,* "the Station of Certainty," which includes *ʿIlm al-Yaqīn,* "Certainty of Knowledge," *ʿAyn al-Yaqīn,* "Certainty of Vision," and *Ḥaqīqat al-Yaqīn,* "Certainty of Reality." You enter these three oceans by *dhikrūllāh.* Don't ask how; Allāh will take you from blindness to vision, from deaf to hearing, from dumbness to speaking. When *ināyatullāh,* Allāh's Care comes, even if you are at the bottom of the valley, Allāh will take you to the top of the mountain; that is your recompense that can happen in a moment! It is not like going up a ladder step-by-step and that ladder is endless, so you will never reach; that happens in the blink of an eye!

Grandshaykh ق said, "If you do *dhikrūllāh* in *jamaʿah* or by yourself, you are dressed with one medallion and the next time, you are dressed with another medallion, regardless of what you have done." So when you do *dhikrūllāh* once a week, that cleans whatever you have done the previous week of and the second *dhikr* cleans you again for the next week. It is *nūr ʿalā nūr,* "light upon light." Prophet ﷺ said:

Lā ilāha illa-Llāh ḥuṣnī wa man dakhala ḥuṣnī āman min ʿadhābī.
Lā ilāha illa-Llāh is My fortress; whoever enters it, is safe from My punishment.
(Ibn Najjār)

Let us say altogether, *lā ilāha illa-Llāh Muḥammadun Rasūlullāh! Lā ilāha illa-Llāh Muḥammadun Rasūlullāh! Lā ilāha illa-Llāh Muḥammadun Rasūlullāh!* We are sending that to our shaykhs to present to Prophet, and for Prophet in his holy grave to present on our behalf on the Day of Judgment.

Qul Allāh thumma dharhum fi khawdihim yalʿabūn.
Say, "Allāh," then leave them to play in their vain discussions.
(Sūrat al-'Anʿām, 6:91)

You can recite it (or pronounce it) as *qul Allāh,* "say 'Allāh'". How do they say there is no *dhikr bi 'Ism adh-Dhāt?* Wahabis say, "Don't do *dhikr* by Allāh's Name." Allāh is saying in Sūrat al-Anām, verse 91, "Leave them playing with what they are doing. You say, 'Allāh.'" We say "Allāh" because we are following the way of our *shuyūkh* and by the order of Allāh in Holy Qur'an. Say "Allāh," as we are ordered! Maybe they are saying, "Shayṭān, Shayṭān" (as their *dhikr*)! And they don't use beads. Allāh said in Holy Qur'an, "Say, 'Allāh.'" Therefore we are saying "Allāh," *dhikr* by *'Ism adh-Dhāt*. It is important in the Naqshbandi Way.

May Allāh ﷻ forgive us and may Allāh ﷻ bless us.

Wa min Allāhi 't-tawfiq, bi ḥurmati 'l-ḥabīb, bi ḥurmati 'l-Fātiḥah.
And with Allāh is success. For the sake of the Beloved, for his sake we recite the opening chapter of Holy Qur'an.

The Oceans of Sayyidina Ali and Sayyidina Abu Bakr

A'ūdhu billāhi min ash-Shayṭāni 'r-rajīm. Bismillāhi' r-Raḥmāni 'r-Raḥīm. Nawaytu 'l-arbā'īn, nawaytu 'l-'itikāf, nawaytu'l-khalwah, nawaytu 'l-'uzlah, nawaytu 'r-riyāḍa, nawaytu 's-sulūk, lillāhi Ta'alā fī hādhā 'l-masjid. Atī'ūllāha wa atī'ū 'r-Rasūla wa ūli 'l-amri minkum. (4:59)

The connection of the heart is very important, and that is why Allāh ﷻ said in Holy Qur'an, "Don't follow those whose hearts we made heedless from Our remembrance." (al-Kahf, 18:28) That means keep you heart always in remembrance of Allāh, keep that connection from when you took *baya'*; the fitting in the pipe is there, but don't lose that connection, don't be heedless! You are forgetting there is a connection from you to the shaykh and from the shaykh to Prophet.

> *Afalā yatadabarūna al-qur'ān aw 'alā qulūbihim aqfāluhā.*
> *Do they not then earnestly seek to understand the Qur'an, or are their hearts locked up by them?* (Sūrat Muḥammad, 47:24)

> *Inna naḥnu nazalnā 'dh-dhikri wa inna lahu la-ḥāfiẓūn.*
> *Verily, We sent down the dhikr and surely, We will guard it (from corruption).* (Sūrat al-Ḥijr, 15:9)

Or are there locks on their hearts? They don't want to remember Allāh. Keep remembering Allāh, as He has said in Sūrat al-Ikhlāṣ, *Qul Hūwa Allāhu Āḥad,* "Say, 'He is Allāh, *Āḥad*; no one is Creator except Him!'" Don't let them have locks on their hearts or be heedless. It is said *al-qulūb awwi'atun wa idhā umlīyat imma al-ḥaqq wa imma al-bāṭil,* "Hearts are containers." The heart is a container that has to be filled; either you fill it with Ḥaqq, Truth, or you fill it with *bāṭil,* falsehood. Fill it with Truth and with Allāh's remembrance, as He said, "Don't let your heart have a lock; I am giving you *dhikrūllāh* to fill it."

And when it is overflowing as you fill it, when it reaches the top, what happens? It will overflow. When you fill the cup slowly, slowly, don't stop here and say, "I am not seeing anything," there is nothing need to see, you don't need to see because it is not for you to ask for something, it is for Allāh, as Rābiʿah al-ʿAdawiyyah ق said, "I am not worshiping from the fear of Hellfire, and not for the love of Paradise, but I am worshipping for Your love, *yā* Allāh, so put me where You like!"

So don't stop filling, fill and keep going, keep going, and when you reach to the top, fill more. Then Shayṭān will come and say to you, "You are crazy, you wasted your time." If you don't listen, then keep going, then it overflows. At that time the light that was inside, when filling up, you can't see it, it is veiled, but when it overflows, it comes outside and that light of *dhikrūllāh's* light will overflow to all the parts of the body. And that happened in Lama in a moment, in one blink of an eye you will see that overflow of the heat and that is not easy to get. You have to struggle very hard against the ego. We are all struggling, as Grandshaykh ق said, *thumma āmanū thumma kafarū*, "One day up, one day down."

There are two ways to fill our containers: one is to fill it with *dhikrūllāh,* to not be heedless, and to not put a lock; and the other way is to do what Shayṭān wants and fill it with *dunyā,* and then all this darkness will come out of the heart and spread through the whole body. So our duty is not to let darkness fill our hearts, but rather to make that light of *dhikrūllāh* come out. Allāh is Merciful with *Ummat an-Nabī;* He said, "Remember Me, I remember you." *wa lā dhikrūllāhi akbar*, "And Allāh's remembrance of you is greater." It cannot be expressed or described; it is over limits.

Sahl ibn ʿAbdAllāh ﷺ said, "It is forbidden, *ḥarām,* on a heart that the light of reality will enter in it." Because maybe that heart has in it something that Allāh ﷻ hates. What does Allāh hate? When you deny His mercy! Then Allāh is not happy, because He wants you to know He is All-Merciful and then He rewards you. And who is His mercy?

> *Wa ma arslanāka illa Raḥmatan lil-ʿĀlamīn.*
> *And We have sent you not (O Muḥammad) but as a mercy for ʿĀlamīn (all the worlds).* (Sūrat al-Anbīyā, 21:107)

That is His Prophet! So you must be happy because you don't deny Allāh's mercy, His Prophet. But those who deny Sayyīdinā Muḥammad ﷺ must repent, as Allāh is not happy with them. We say, *"As-salām ʿalayk, yā Rasūlullāh*! We love you and hope to be with you on Judgment Day. We love our *shuyūkh* and Mawlana Shaykh, and we love your family!"

And az-Zuhrī ﷺ said, *ṣalāḥ al-qulūb afḍal min ʿibādati 'th-thaqalayn,* "To remedy the heart for one hour is better than the worship of Sayyīdinā Adam ﷺ up to the Day of Judgment." That means sitting in *dhikrūllāh* for one hour is better than the worship of *ins* and *jinn* from day one to the end of *dunyā*!

That is one *walī* describing how much he is getting through his experiences through one hour. Imagine then in *khalwah* how much you are doing *dhikrūllāh*! They allow only two hours of sleep. When given permission for *khalwah,* you feel you don't need to eat or sleep as you have power. So you read Qur'an and mention Allāh's Beautiful Names and Attributes, and that is *dhikrūllāh*. That is worth more than all the combined worship of *ins* and *jinn*. When Allāh sees you devoting and doing that remembrance, He will give you from His mercy! That means He will give to you from Sayyīdinā Muḥammad ﷺ, and when that happens you see things and hear things that never occurred before!

It is said that in our way the only condition that the shaykh takes from the *murīd* is to leave forbiddens. That is why Grandshaykh ق said, "There are 800 forbiddens that we have to take away from ourselves, and to leave one forbidden is better than the worship of the *ins* and *jinn*." You will be rewarded more than that worship. It doesn't mean you have to leave your prayers, obligations are required; we are not talking about that. Beyond that Allāh gives you, *ma lā ʿaynun rā'at wa lā udhunun samiʿat wa lā khaṭar ʿalā qalbi bashar,* "What no eye saw and no ear heard and what no one can understand of what Allāh give of reward for leaving one forbidden."

The Merit of Leaving a Forbidden Habit

That is more valuable, to leave one of the 800 forbiddens than to do all the 500 *māmurāt,* all the forms of worship. Why? Because you are letting your heart's container be filled with the lights that Allāh wants there and not letting Iblīs take it from you! What did Sayyīdinā ʿAlī ﷺ say? We know this kind of knowledge is coming from two sources to the Prophet ﷺ, one is Sayyīdinā ʿAlī ﷺ and one is through Abū Bakr aṣ-Ṣiddīq ق. Sayyīdinā ʿAlī came to the Prophet and this is not a *ḥadīth,* but it was mentioned by Sayyīdinā Ali, *dhu nafs ar-radiyya. Dullanī ʿalā aqrab aṭ-ṭuruq il-Allāh wa afḍaluhā,* "Guide me to easiest, nearest of ways to Allāh and the most easy one."

Because there is a *ḥadīth* that one *Ṣaḥābī* ⬥ came to Prophet and said, *qad kathurat ʿalay sharīʿah al-Islām*, "I am a person who is weak. There are too many obligations in Islam and there are too many rules." That is why people today are so dipped in the oceans of liberalism and love of *dunyā* that they cannot accept more than the easy way. They don't want to be *awlīyā* and that relationship with Allāh is forgotten.

ʿAlā inna awlīyāullāh la khawfan ʿalayhim wa lā hum yaḥzanūn.
Verily, on the friends of Allāh there is no fear, nor shall they grieve.
(Sūrat Yūnus, 10:62)

As one scholar said, "Wear jeans, pray your prayers and then go to the mall. That is enough for you." No, that is not enough! As we said, leaving a forbidden is better than the worship of *jinn* and *ins,* and that *Ṣaḥābī* ⬥ asked for something to make easy for him Islam. And Prophet ﷺ said, "Keep your tongue wet with *dhikrūllāh*." And is that difficult or easy? It is easy!

Wadhkur rabbaka fī nafsika taḍaruʿan wa khufiyā wa dūn al-jahri min al-qawl wa lā takun mina 'l-ghāfilīn.
And bring your Lord to remembrance in your (very) soul, with humility and in reverence, without loudness in words, in the mornings and evenings, and be not of those who are unheedful. (Sūrat al-Aʿrāf, 7:205)

"Remember Allāh in yourself or in your heart, or don't make it loud." That means keep it in your heart. Don't let Shayṭān enter your heart, let Allāh enter your heart! Then, "I will let My lights and manifestations enter your heart." So that *Ṣaḥābī* ⬥ wanted something easy and so Prophet said, "Do *dhikrūllāh* through your tongue," as doing heart *dhikr* is more difficult. So Sayyīdinā ʿAlī ⬥ said, "Guide me to a way to Allāh that is easiest." And the Prophet said, *ʿalayka bi dawāmati dhikrillāh fil-khalwah*, "Your duty is to remember Allāh ﷻ in your seclusion, when you are alone." It means keep Allāh's remembrance always; when you are able, do it. "In *khalwah*" means in secrecy, not like the *Ṣaḥābī* who asked the Prophet ﷺ and he said, "Keep your tongue busy with *dhikrullah*." For Sayyīdinā ʿAlī it is higher, "Keep doing *dhikrūllāh* in hidden way to fill your heart with *dhikrūllāh*."

That means your heart has to be with Allāh, but your face, *dhāhir*, has to be with the people, as the Prophet said, *lī saʿatun maʿ Allāh wa saʿatun maʿ al-khalq*, "I have one hour with Allāh and one hour with people." Or, "One face with Allāh and one face with people." And so you keep that secret. Where do you keep secrets? You lock them up in the heart. And how do you lock them after you do *dhikr*? It is as Mawlana Shaykh and Grandshaykh ق taught us to recite, *awda'na hādha adh-dhikr 'indak, yā Rasūlullāh,* "We have placed this *dhikr* in your presence, O Messenger of Allāh!" to hand it off to Prophet for him to keep for us, or else we will lose it slowly, slowly to Shayṭān. "*Yā Rasūlullāh!* We immediately deposit that prayer or *du'ā* or *dhikr* in your bank, before we spend it!" You can easily spend it when Shayṭān comes. He says, "I give you this, I give you *dunyā*," and you lose it.

And Sayyīdinā 'Alī ☙ asked, *kayfa adhkur, yā Rasūlullāh,* "How do I do that *dhikr*; what is the technique or way?" He said, *ghammi 'aynayk,* "Close your eyes and listen three times what I am going to say." Why did he say, "Close your eyes." That means, "Disconnect yourself completely from *dunyā.*"

Inna as-sama' wal-basar wal-fu'ād kullu ulaika kāna 'anha masūla.
And pursue not that of which thou hast no knowledge; for every act of hearing, or of seeing or of (feeling in) the heart will be enquired into (on the Day of Reckoning). (Sūrat al-'Isrā', 17:36)

May Allāh ﷻ forgive us, by us saying, "*Yā Rasūlullāh,* we love you!" *Allāh, Allāh. 'alā kull man taghā wa tajabbar 'alā anfusinā.*

So the biggest connection to *dunyā* is what? It is the eyes. With ears you hear but you cannot see. So to see is through the eyes, and when *awlīyāullāh* want to attract *murīds* it is through their eyes. They attract people when they look into their eyes. When they look into their eyes then that shaykh will carry them. So that is what we mentioned about Shaykh Sharafuddīn ق and Grandshaykh ق. They went to a mall in Istanbul to make people to look at their eyes. As an ironic thing, seeing these two shaykh with their two turbans and seeing that and smiling and laughing, that is a joke. And they look into their eyes and as soon as they do that they carry them, attract them.

So eyes are very important for *awlīyā*. When you look into the eyes of people that attracts them and one day Allāh will guide them.

Inna ad-dīn 'indāllāh al-Islām.
The religion before Allāh is Islām. (Sūrat 'Āli 'Imrān, 3:19)

So he said, "Close your eyes and repeat three times." When you close your eyes, where are you? Away from *dunyā* and with the One you mention. And he said to him, "Say, *'lā ilāha illa-Llāh Muḥammadun Rasūlullāh.'*" And Sayyīdinā ʿAlī was hearing. *Aghmid ʿaynayk wa asmaʿ*. So do both, disconnect from *dunyā* and close your eyes and enter the garden of the Divine Presence, and though you might not see anything, of course Sayyīdinā ʿAlī was seeing, but we listen to *lā ilāha illa-Llāh.*

> *Faʿlam annahu lā ilāha illa-Llāh w'astaghfir li-dhanbik wa li 'l-mu'minīna wa 'l-mu'mināti w 'Allāhu yaʿlamu muqallibukum wa mathwākum.*
> *Know, therefore, that there is no god but Allāh, and ask forgiveness for your faults, and for the men and women who believe, for Allāh knows how you move about and how you dwell in your homes.* (Sūrat Muḥammad, 47:19)

"Know that there is no Creator except Me. When you carry that power, I am giving that power," and then, *astaghfir li dhanbik wa li 'l-mu'minīna wa 'l-mu'mināti,* "Then ask forgiveness for believers." That is the biggest power that Allāh gave to *Ummat an-Nabī*. Allāh will be happy with that *lā ilāha illa-Llāh, Maqām at-Tawḥīd*. You are declaring there is none to be worshiped except Allāh!

That is the message of Islam, you have to know there is no Creator except Allāh ﷻ. And if you say *lā ilāha illa-Llāh,* that is the most powerful tool. And then Sayyīdinā ʿAlī ؓ closed his eyes and repeated what the Prophet said. So at that moment when you say that *dhikr,* the Prophet is present and that is the *dhikr* that Prophet ﷺ taught Sayyīdinā ʿAli. So Sayyīdinā ʿAlī is present, and that takes you to the Divine Presence and you might not see that but Allāh is witness that you are saying to Him, "There is none to worship except You!"

So that is the tool that was given to Sayyīdinā ʿAlī and we are saying, "O Allāh! We are accepting that tool to remember You all the time in our life and if we are forgetting to do that, we ask You to send angels to do that on our behalf!!" And Prophet ﷺ is the city of knowledge and ʿAlī is its door. So that is the loud *dhikr* given to Sayyīdinā ʿAlī and that is through every *ṭarīqah* that comes from him, the door to it is that *dhikr*. So the other door to Prophet is Sayyīdinā Abū Bakr aṣ-Ṣiddīq and the method of Sayyīdinā Abū Bakr is a different way. Those coming through the Naqshbandi Way are combining the two ways from the prophet of Sayyīdinā Abū Bakr ق and

Sayyīdinā 'Alī ⸎, and they combine in Sayyīdinā Jafar aṣ-Ṣadiq ق. He was one of the twelve *imāms* of Islam and they were coming from time to time, and Sayyīdinā Jafar combined in him those two sources, as mentioned in the Qur'an:

Maraj al-baḥrayni yaltaqīyān.
He has let free the two bodies of flowing water, meeting together.

(Sūrat ar-Raḥmān, 55:19)

The word "merge" comes from Arabic, does it not? *SubḥānAllāh*, the English language takes from the Holy Qur'an; also in French, "merger," takes from the Holy Qur'an. So, *marraj al-baḥrayn yaltaqīyān*, "The two oceans are merging," the ocean of Sayyīdinā 'Alī ⸎ and the ocean of Sayyīdinā Abū Bakr ⸎. That is the Golden Ocean whose value cannot be described!

That is why we say, *lā ilāha illa-Llāh, lā ilāha illa-Llāh, lā ilāha illa-Llāh*. That is why we said yesterday to people on the Internet who were typing, "*Allāh, Allāh, Allāh, Allāh...*" that is an electromagnetic voice that goes forever and you will be continuously rewarded! *Dhikr* of *lā ilāha illa-Llāh* leads to Allāh!

May Allāh ⸎ forgive us and may Allāh ⸎ bless us.

Wa min Allāhi 't-tawfīq, bi ḥurmati 'l-ḥabīb, bi ḥurmati 'l-Fātiḥah.
And with Allāh is success. For the sake of the Beloved, for his sake we recite the opening chapter of Holy Qur'an.

The Four Levels of Dhikr and the Heart of Sayyidina Ali

Aʿūdhu billāhi min ash-Shayṭāni 'r-rajīm. Bismillāhi' r-Raḥmāni 'r-Raḥīm.
Nawaytu 'l-arbāʿīn, nawaytu 'l-ʿitikāf, nawaytu'l-khalwah, nawaytu 'l-ʿuzlah,
nawaytu 'r-riyāḍa, nawaytu 's-sulūk, lillāhi Taʿalā fī hādhā 'l-masjid.
Atīʿūllāha wa atīʿū 'r-Rasūla wa ūli 'l-amri minkum. (4:59)

We must always remember to ask *madad* from our shaykh, and he is taking *madad* from Prophet, whom Allāh made *khalīfah* of this Creation and a Mercy for all the Worlds, *Raḥmatan lil-ʿĀlamīn,* which can also be *Raḥmatan lil-ʿĀlamayn,* "Mercy for the Two Worlds," and sometimes scholars explain *ʿalamayn* as, "Mankind and *jinn.*" So there is *mulk,* this world's Creation, and *malakūt,* Heavenly Creation. He is mercy for both. And no one knows when Allāh ﷻ created His Beloved Prophet ﷺ. From him *ʿUlūm al-Awwalīn wal-ʿĀkhirīn,* Knowledge of Before and After, is coming. So we cannot say other than that Prophet ﷺ is *khalīfah* on Earth and in Heavens.

May Allāh keep us always in Presence of Prophet. To him there are doors that you can enter, big or small, but there are doors. *Awlīyā* know the doors. We mentioned yesterday the importance of the door of Sayyīdinā ʿAli, *karam-Allāhu wajaha,* and how Prophet ﷺ taught him to make *dhikrūllāh* with *lā ilāha illa-Llāh.* It is also mentioned in many books of previous *awlīyāullāh* and by Grandshaykh ق and Mawlana Shaykh Nazim, may Allāh give him long life, that *dhikrūllāh* is of different kinds and has different levels.

One of them is *dhikr al-lisān, "dhikr* of the tongue", to keep your tongue always in remembrance of Allāh ﷻ and always mentioning His Beautiful Names and Attributes, which allows you to enter that Reality. By always doing that *dhikr* of *lā ilāha illa-Llāh,* it is the sword against our bad *ʿamal,* deeds. Ego always likes to be something. That *dhikr* is telling us, "Don't listen to or believe your ego, as Shayṭān can play with it."

So before going to Abū Bakr aṣ-Ṣiddīq's door, we say one of the types of *dhikr* is *dhikr al-lisān, Dhikr* of the Tongue, which is considered the first step to enter the Ocean of Heavens. That is why *awlīyā* can understand that from the verse:

Maraja al-baḥrayni yaltaqīyāni baynahumā barzakhun lā yabghiyān.
He has let loose the two seas meeting together. Between them is a barrier which none of them can transgress. (Sūrat ar-Raḥmān, 55:19-20)

That *barzakh* is an area of quarantine; it stops one ocean overtaking the other. If you want to pass from one ocean to another you have to enter that area, *barzakh*, and wait until they are ready to let you go to the other ocean. This happens among sea creatures. Scientists discovered that the Mediterranean and Atlantic Oceans don't mix, and between them is, to us, an imaginary line, but fish sense that line and stop at it to enter that quarantine. When they are ready, they move to the other ocean.

It means with those with *dhikr al-lisān* are in the ocean of Sayyīdinā ʿAli, and that is why we begin with *lā ilāha illa-Llāh,* and when we finish that, in the Naqshbandi Order, we go to *dhikr* of "Allāh". This is in *jamaʿat,* but when we do *dhikr* alone we begin with "Allāh". In *jamaʿat,* in a technical sense, we are all moving from one ocean to another ocean so we have to come with *lā ilāha illa-Llāh, lā ilāha illa-Llāh, lā ilāha illa-Llāh, lā ilāha illa-Llāh,* and we are approaching the area where we have to go, before entering the ocean of Abū Bakr aṣ-Ṣiddīq. So you stop there, and they check whether are you able to go on or whether you need quarantine. You enter the quarantine area and they will keep you there until you are ready to go into the other ocean by remembrance of *ʿIsm adh-Dhāt*, "Allāh".

That is why it is said, *falzam dhikr adh-Dhāt*, until you reach the other ocean, the *dhikr* of Paradise, D*hikr ul-Jinān* is through *ʿIsm adh-Dhāt*, "Allāh".

Dhikr of *lā ilāha illa-Llāh* takes you from *dunyā* and it states Allāh's Oneness, to show humanity, "There is no god but Allāh." That is denial of the ego and Shayṭān, and denial of anyone who associates anything with Allāh. Allāh is The One Who saves you, from Hell and from punishment, and sends you to be with Sayyīdinā Muḥammad ﷺ! That takes you from *dunyā* to the remembrance of Allāh, so then you are entering *Jannah,* Paradise. That is why it is called *dhikrūllāh: Allāh, Allāh, Allāh,* is *dhikr* of the heart, which is *dhikr* of Paradise!

So that is why in the Naqshbandi Order the first step they take, the shaykh will carry you with his power and lead you by your hand, and you will that through quarantine in the blink of an eye! Then he puts you in that ocean of *ʿIsm adh-Dhāt.* And that is why the Naqshbandi begin with *dhikr* of *ʿIsm adh-Dhāt,* sitting by themselves quietly, going from 1500 times daily recitation to 5,000 to 10,000 times, as much as you can.

Grandshaykh ق said, "O *'IbādAllāh,* Servants of Allāh! *Faqsud hum washtanshiqhum... arwāḥi 'ṭ-ṭayyib.* Run to these Naqshbandi shaykhs and smell their beauty and smell their sweat, as their sweat is the sweat of love in the Divine Presence! You are never going to smell such a fragrance and you can never imagine how nice it is! Through that smell, *fatafūz 'alā hadhal-jawhar an-nafis,* you are going to be able to attain that beautiful diamond that takes away all obstacles on your way. And their way, the Naqshbandi Way, is the easiest way. They don't let the *murīd* go hungry, and don't make the *murīd* stay awake all night. Moderation is their way. They are always moderate and they don't put you under too much pressure, as Allāh ﷻ said:

> *Lā yukallifullāh nafsan illā wus'aha.*
> *On no soul does Allāh place a burden greater than it can bear.*
> (Sūrat al-Baqarah, 2:286)

So they prepare you according to your capacity in a moderate way so that you go quickly. And every *masjid* is a *zāwīya* for them; they can do their *dhikr* anywhere and no one can asks them what they you doing, as they are doing silent, *khafī, dhikr.* And their hearts are always with their Lord.

> *Wa man dakhalahu kāna āminan w 'alā an-nāsi hajj al-bayt man istaṭa'a ilayhi sabīlā.*
> *Whoever enters the House of Allāh is safe, and pilgrimage to the House of Allāh is a duty on Mankind (who are able).* (Sūrat 'Āli 'Imrān, 3:97)

How to Reach Safety

Safety is there as you enter His House, so whoever enters it is in safety. Allāh ﷻ said to Prophet ﷺ directly in *Ḥadīth Qudsī:*

> *Ma wasi'anī ardī wa lā samā'ī wa lākin wasi'anī qalbī 'abdī al-mu'min.*
> *My Earth did not contain Me, nor My Heavens, but the heart of My believing servant contained Me.*

So that means if you let your soul enter the heart, and the ego has been cut down, at that time your soul and spirit can enter your heart, and then you find safety. That is why *awlīyā* found safety, because their ego has been prevented from entering their hearts. But by listening and obeying, and through love and respect, Allāh cut their ego down and made an easy way for them to enter their hearts and then when they enter they are safe, *wa man dakhalahu kāna āminan w ʿalā an-nāsi hajj al-bayt man istaṭaʿa ilayhi sabīlā.*

There is an obligation to visit the House of Allāh, and as a believer, like visiting the House of Allāh in *Meccatu 'l-Mukarrama,* you have to visit the "House of the Heart". When you circumambulate the heart, you circumambulate the Light that Allāh ﷻ is sending to your heart.

Allāh wants His servants to visit His House; those who are able, *istitaʿa 'ilayh sabīla,* are in reality those who step on their ego, not those who are happy in *dunyā* doing what they like, who say, "It is enough that we pray." Okay, you have to pray, but you cannot open the door of the house to those lights without stepping on your ego. *Dhikrūllāh* is the key to that door of that house with that light! Who entered is in safety, and Allāh ﷻ wants you to circumambulate that House, in that kind of movement that expresses your ecstasy.

That is like in *ḥaḍrah,* expressing yourself in that movement, which is similar to circumambulating the House, which is expressing your love. That is not dancing, but going around the House. And at that time, you go around your own House that Allāh made ready for you. And this moves on to why they said that remembrance is of four types in every level.

There are four types of *dhikr* in every level you go to. On the level of *dhikr* of *lā ilāha illa-Llāh* and *dhikr* of *Allāh, Allāh,* there are four types. First is the *dhikr* that you mention. You may mention a Beautiful Name or make *ṣalawāt* or whatever you want. Second is *dhikrun tadhkuru bih, dhikr* in which you mention Allāh; it might be through His Beautiful Names. Third is *dhikru tadhkuruk,* the *dhikr* that mentions you. Fourth is *dhikr yadhkuru bika, dhikr* in which you will be mentioned.

The first one is *dhikrun tadhkuruhu, dhikr tatrud al-ghaflah,* the *dhikr* that throws away heedlessness. You are doing something good to throw away your heedlessness. The second is *tadhkur madhdkūrun imma al-ʿadhāb aw imma al-qurb,* the *dhikr* that brings you near and saves you from punishment. The third is *wa dhikrun yadhkuruka.* "Remember Me and will I remember you," so when you mention Him through His Beautiful Names, Allāh mentions you in return. The fourth is, *hūw dhikrūllāhi li ʿabdihi wa laysa li ʿabdihi mutaʿallaq,* "Allāh mentions His servant without His servant having done anything."

Without His servant mentioning His Names, His love, punishment or reward, there is a *dhikr* that remembers you! Who is "you"?

Inna Allāh wa malā'ikatahu yūṣallūn ʿalā an-nabī yā ayyuhalladhīna āmanū ṣallū ʿalayhi wa sallimū taslīmā.
Allāh and His angels send blessings on the Prophet: O you that believe! Send blessings on him, and salute him with all respect. (Sūrat al-'Aḥzāb, 33:56)

That is the one that without him mentioning Allāh, He mentioned him. That is *wahbana,* a grant from Allāh. Nothing is a cause of what He does, or what the Prophet did, it is a direct grant from Allāh. That is why *awlīyāullāh* say that representatives of Prophet have been chosen without them doing anything; he takes one and says, "You are Prophet's representative." Allāh mentioned him. Who can dispute this? That is the highest *dhikrūllāh,* that He mentioned them.

And *awlīyā* are lucky, as because of Prophet they are mentioned. *Inna Allāh wa malā'ikatahu yuṣallūn ʿalā an-nabī.* It means, "Follow My Way by doing as I do, and send *ṣalawāt* on Prophet. Then you are following what I ordered in Holy Qur'an:

Qul in kuntum tuḥibbūn-Allāha fattabiʿūnī yuḥbibkumu Allāhu wa yaghfir lakum dhunūbakum w'Allāhu Ghafūrun Raḥīm.
Say, "If you love Allāh, follow me (Muḥammad). Allāh will love you and forgive you your sins, for Allāh is Oft-Forgiving, Most Merciful."
(Sūrat ʻĀli ʻImrān, 3:31)

Say to them, O Muḥammad, "If you really love Allāh, then follow and love me, and then I will love you."

And the Prophet ﷺ said, "When I love you, then Allāh loves you." That is why Prophet made it easy for us by saying, "Follow my son-in-law and cousin. I am the city of knowledge and ʿAlī is its door; open the door and enter through that way. If you want the other way, the hidden way, I am giving you Abū Bakr aṣ-Ṣiddīq." That is why it is said by many different *awlīyā* and scholars, it is certain that when Allāh mentioned Abū Bakr aṣ-Ṣiddīq in Holy Qur'an, when they were in the cave, Prophet ﷺ said, 'O Abū Bakr! Don't be sad.'"

Illa tanṣu Rūḥu faqad naṣarahu Allāhu idh akhrajahu alladhīna kafarū thanīyy ithnayni idh humā fi 'l-ghāri idh yaqūlu li-ṣāḥibihi lā taḥzan inna allāha maʿanā fa-anzalā Allāhu sakīnatahu ʿalayhi wa ayyadahu bi-junūdin lam tarawhā wa jaʿalā kalimata 'Lladhīna kafarū 's-sufla wa kalimatullāhi hīya al-ʿulyā wa 'Llāhu ʿAzīzun Ḥakīm.

The second of two, when they (Prophet and Abū Bakr) were in the cave, and he said to his companion, "Be not sad (or afraid), for surely Allāh is with us." Then Allāh sent down His sakīnah (calmness, tranquility, peace) upon him, and strengthened him with forces which you saw not.(Sūrat at-Tawbah, 9:40)

Why Enter the Cave?

Which cave? Yes, we know it was *Ghāri Thawr*, when they were migrating from Mecca to Madinah, hiding. Hiding from what? Does Prophet need to hide? He went for *Mi'rāj*, so who can touch him? But he entered there for a certain reason: to pass that authority to Sayyīdinā Abū Bakr aṣ-Ṣiddīq, that knowledge Allāh is sending, *anzalā Allāhu sakīnatahu 'alayh*, He manifest His tranquility, peacefulness, love, mercy on them. It means when they entered the Cave of Sayyīdinā Muḥammad ﷺ, it is like *as-ḥāb al-Kahf*, the "Companions of the Cave." Where did they enter?

Fa awū il al-kahf yanshur lakum rabbukum min raḥmatih wa yuhayyi lakum min amrikum mirfaqā.
Betake yourselves to the Cave. Your Lord will shower His mercies on you and disposes of your affair towards comfort and ease." (Sūrat al-Kahf, 18:62)

"Run to the cave, O People of the Cave!" Who is in that cave? That is Sayyīdinā Muḥammad ﷺ! It's also like when He ordered them to enter the *fulk al-mashhūn*:

Wa khalaqnā lahum min mithlihi mā yarkabūn.
And We have created for them similar (vessels) on which they ride.
(Sūrat al-YāSīn, 36:42)

Sayyīdinā Nūḥ put everyone in that ark, *fulk al-mashhūn*, the boat of Sayyīdinā Nūḥ is like the heart of Sayyīdinā Muḥammad ﷺ. Literally it is the boat of Sayyīdinā Nūḥ, but it is also an indication that if you run to that boat you will be in safety. "And We have created something similar to it in which you can ride." And what is similar to that boat? Where that boat is Sayyīdinā Muḥammad ﷺ, the ones similar is Sayyīdinā Abū Bakr aṣ-Ṣiddīq and Sayyīdinā 'Ali, and *awlīyā*, according to their levels, to take *Ummat an-Nabī* to safety.

So that is why Sayyīdinā Abū Bakr ﷺ entered the boat and the cave, and Allāh sent that *sakīnah* on them, that peacefulness, and He defeated their enemies for them, meaning, the enemy that attacks and whispers in ears of people, Shayṭān. So those who entered with Sayyīdinā Abū Bakr aṣ-Ṣiddīq are going to be with him in that cave and they were present, and generation after generation and century after century, those receiving their sainthood from Abū Bakr aṣ-Ṣiddīq have authority to bring people to safety. Through their power and their spotlight they attract people to safety.

About Sayyīdinā ʿAli ﷺ, Prophet ﷺ said, "I am the city of knowledge and ʿAlī is its door." So what did Sayyīdinā ʿAlī do? He was the door of safety, they were not able to enter the city except through Sayyīdinā ʿAli. He was the guardian for the Prophet ﷺ, although Prophet doesn't need this, but he put these *Ṣaḥābah* ﷺ, about whom he said:

As-hābī ka 'n-nujūm bi ayyihim aqtadaytum ahtadaytum.
My Companions are like stars (on a dark night); whichever of them you follow, you will be guided.[2]

So Sayyīdinā ʿAlī ﷺ was in Prophet's bed when the Quraysh made their conspiracy to kill the Prophet ﷺ. Who went in that bed? Is that a normal bed or something special? That is the bed of prophecy, and he received the secrets of prophecy! When they opened the door and found Sayyīdinā ʿAlī there, they were blocked. That means that no Shayṭān can go through that door! So Sayyīdinā ʿAlī is at the heart of every believer, meaning, "I am the ocean of knowledge in the heart of every believer and ʿAlī is there at the door." That means when you enter the door, you enter the cave, and the door is Sayyīdinā ʿAlī and inside is Sayyīdinā Abū Bakr!

That doesn't mean Abū Bakr is higher than Sayyīdinā ʿAli, or that Sayyīdinā ʿAlī is higher than Sayyīdinā Abū Bakr, nor that they are higher than Sayyīdinā 'Umar. The Prophet ﷺ loves and guides all of them the same, but he might have more family love toward Sayyīdinā ʿAli, as he was his son-in-law and cousin and the first young person to accept Islam.

So that heart of the believer is where Prophet's city is ready, and if you are able to go through Sayyīdinā ʿAlī to that city, you receive what *awlīyā*

---

2 `Abd ibn Humayd, ad-Daraqutnee, ibn `Adiyy, ibn `Abd al-Barr with unsound chains but the meaning is sound.

receive. May Allāh open that city for us! Whoever enters it is safe. That means safety is in that city, and in that heart which Allāh ﷻ gave you. Every heart is different; in some hearts that city will expand and be huge, and in some it will be smaller, depending on the capacity of each one. Next time we will go into what Prophet put in Sayyīdinā Abū Bakr's heart.

May Allāh ﷻ forgive us and may Allāh ﷻ bless us.

Wa min Allāhi 't-tawfiq, bi ḥurmati 'l-ḥabīb, bi ḥurmati 'l-Fātiḥah.
And with Allāh is success. For the sake of the Beloved, for his sake we recite the opening chapter of Holy Qur'an.

To Kiss the Holy Threshold of Prophet[3]

A'ūdhu billāhi min ash-Shayṭāni 'r-rajīm. Bismillāhi' r-Raḥmāni 'r-Raḥīm. Nawaytu 'l-arbā'īn, nawaytu 'l-'itikāf, nawaytu'l-khalwah, nawaytu 'l-'uzlah, nawaytu 'r-riyāḍa, nawaytu 's-sulūk, lillāhi Ta'alā fī hādhā 'l-masjid. Atī'ūllāha wa atī'ū 'r-Rasūla wa ūli 'l-amri minkum. (4:59)

One day I decided to visit Madinat al-Munawwara, because every Thursday and Friday I prayed there as I was living in Jeddah most of the time. I received a call from my shaykh, Mawlana Shaykh Muhammad Nazim al-Haqqani ق.

He said, "Where are you going?"

I answered, "*Yā Sayyidi*! If there is permission, I am going to visit the Prophet ﷺ."

He said, "Kiss his threshold for me."

When someone says something like that to you, especially your shaykh, your mind begins to think, "How am I going to do that with all those barriers and guards? It is impossible."

When the Prophet ﷺ went into *'Isrā* and *Mi'rāj*—and this is a problem many of us are facing today and the answer and the meaning of spirituality comes with this story. Spirituality is not something you have to do, but it is in addition to giving charity, fasting, praying and making Hajj. It is the way to reach *Maqām al-Ihsān* as mentioned in the *ḥadīth* of Sayyīdinā 'Umar ؓ, that to reach state of *Ihsān*, Moral Excellence, you have to fulfill the Five Pillars of Islam and accept the six Pillars of *Iman* and the principles of how to reach the state of *Ihsān*.

That is very complex and difficult to do and if you say, "I will go to that station by myself," you will only turn in circles. You must have a guide to reach that spiritual station, and if you seek them you will find them, the saints who are brothers and all of them love each other. I am not speaking about false saints, but about real saints that give their lives for their students.

3 From a 2008 *suḥbah*.

So that time I went and was driving about 120 miles per hour in order to reach quickly, because Mawlana said, "Go and kiss the threshold of the Prophet ﷺ," so there must be an opening. I reached there quickly by the *barakah* of the Prophet ﷺ and then had to take a shower and go that holy place that Allah made *qata'n min al-jannah*, a piece of Paradise! At the *Muwajaha*, the holy place of Paradise (it is heavy on my heart to say 'grave'), one tries to stay as long as you can and you don't want to go out! When we visit the Prophet ﷺ, it is *adab* to stand as much as we can in his presence, even not making *du'a*, but only standing there trying to connect our heart with his heart in a way that:

> *Tafakkarru sa'atin khayrun min 'ibādati saba'īn sannah.*
> *To remember Allah ﷻ (contemplate or meditate) for one hour is better than seventy years of worship.*

That is for one hour when you are contemplating by yourself, so how do you think it is when in the holy presence of the Prophet ﷺ? When passing there everyone might stand five minutes, seven minutes, ten minutes and then go. Some might stand more and more and more, it depends on how much they are in that connection. So with the guidance of our *shuyukh*, we have visited the Prophet ﷺ with Mawlana Shaykh Nazim many times and may Allah give him long life. Back in times when there were no barriers, I saw Mawlana Shaykh stand there and make *du'a* for 90 minutes! It was really more like a conversation. You feel you don't see that as you need a lot to reach that level of *mushāhadah*, but you can feel the holy presence.

Mawlana Shaykh Nazim ق stood there for one-and-a-half hours and then he moved to the place of Abū Bakr aṣ-Ṣiddīq ق and stood another half hour, and then to Sayyīdinā 'Umar ق another half hour, and then to Bāb Jibrīl, *mahbit al-wahī* (where Sayyīdinā Jibrīl ﷺ came with *wahī* to the Prophet ﷺ), and then we went back to the *maqām* of Sayyida Fatimah az-Zahra ؏, which Grandshaykh ق said the angels moved her holy body to the end to the place where Sayyīdinā 'Isa ﷺ is to be buried. That is why *awlīyāullāh* see Sayyida Fatima there. Mawlana spent 45 minutes there and then went to *Bab at-Tawbah* (now closed), where he made a special *du'a* and *sajda*.

You have to take the opportunity when it is presented, and whatever was in my heart I was making sure to take that opportunity! Normally, many guards tell you to move and I don't stand at the beginning, the closest area; I normally stand further away, near the wall. However, that night, although there were many guards, one of them with a red beard was the head guard and he didn't approach me nor allow any guard to come to me. It was strange, because you cannot stand there one hour or one-and-a-half hours as they will tell you to move even after five minutes.

So I finished and went to kiss the big pillar in the back as no one will see you there, then one of the big head guards approached me and I said to myself, "It is finished now." He came to me and said, "Do you want to kiss the threshold of the Prophet ﷺ?" I said yes, and he took me to the door of the Prophet ﷺ and I was able to kiss the holy threshold, and everything disappeared: there were no guards and I saw nothing but the threshold of the Prophet ﷺ! I kissed it and stood up, and then everything came back as normal.

That guard said, "Give my *salāms* to Shaykh Nazim." He never knew Mawlana Shaykh Nazim, and Shaykh Nazim never called him and he never called Shaykh Nazim.

I left and went to *Madrassat ash-Shūnah,* where Mawlana Shaykh Nazim usually goes. There I heard footsteps running behind me and I said to myself, "O, they are coming!" I turned and saw one of the guards approaching and he was holding a very beautiful decorated Qur'an that he gave to me and said, "O Hisham! This is a gift from my father for Shaykh Nazim." I thanked him and didn't say anything, nor did I ask him anything as that is *tark al-adab,* beyond good conduct. *Tariqah* is not to ask anything, but rather to *asmaʿū wa awū,* listen and act on what you heard. So I was so into it as if I was lost. You cannot understand it and I don't understand it even now. You cannot use your mind in such situations.

> *Thumma arjiʿi 'l-basara karratayni yanqalib ilayka 'l-basaru khāsiyan wa huwa hasīr.*
> *Then look again and yet again; your sight will return to you weak and made dim.* (Sūrat al-Mulk, 67:4)

Look at one star, twice even! *Yanqalib ilayka 'l-basaru khāsiyan wa huwa hasīr*, your sight returns back defeated from one star, so what do you think about 80 billion stars in our galaxy? What do we know by our mind in the head? We know nothing, but by the mind in our heart we know everything. What did Allah ﷻ say to the Prophet ﷺ and the Prophet ﷺ said to us?

Mā wasiʿanī ardī wa lāsamā'ī wa lākin wasiʿanī qalbi ʿabdī al-mu'min. Neither My Heavens nor My Earth contain Me, but the heart of My believing servant contains Me. (*Ḥadīth Qudsī, Al-Ihya* of Imam al-Ghazali)

It means, "The believer's heart contained My Light, My Attributes[4], the understanding of the universe!" Do you think *awlīyāullāh* don't have power to pass beyond this universe? Prophet ﷺ went beyond this universe, beyond the stars! He ﷺ passed through 80 billion stars in our galaxy and then he passed 60 billion galaxies and even further, to *Qāba Qawsayni aw Adnā,* what might be one centimeter or one millimeter from the Divine Presence!

To Follow in the Prophet's Footsteps

Allah ﷻ said to the prophets, and especially to his saints:

Qul in kuntum tuḥibbūna 'Llāha fattabiʿūnī yuhbibkumullāhu wa yaghfir lakum dhunūbakum w'Allāhu Ghafūru 'r-Raḥīm.
Say (O Muhammad), "If you (really) love Allah, then follow me! Allah will love you and forgive your sins, and Allah is Oft-Forgiving, Most Merciful.
(Sūrat Āli-'Imrān, 3:31)

This is *khās,* understanding for them. Do *awlīyāullāh* follow the Prophet ﷺ or not? We might struggle to follow, but they do not as spiritually they gave up their lives for the Prophet ﷺ. That means to follow the Prophet ﷺ in every step, and if he went for *Miʿrāj* you go for *Miʿrāj,* or else you are not a *walī*. A *walī* <u>must</u> follow in the footsteps of Prophet ﷺ! Does a *walī* love Allah or not? Yes, that is a condition to be a *walī*. That means they are following in the footsteps of Prophet ﷺ and going in *Miʿrāj,* and that is why they can guide, because they are following and learning and giving!

Sayyīdinā Abdul Qadir al-Jilani ق said in his *Fath ar-Rabbani,* "*Yā Ghulām,* O child!" His students were big scholars who sat facing him, the *Ghawth*. He said, "*Yā Ghulām*! You are still a child as you didn't reach maturity yet." That is dangerous, because if we are not mature how are we going to obey or be responsible? You have to understand when he says, "*Yā*

4 Not the Divine Essence.

Ghulām!" There is a secret there because he is the *Ghawth*. I never said that before, although we were going through that book in Ramadan every morning, but they are saying to open this secret now.

So it means you aren't responsible, the *awlīyāullāh* are responsible. If you take the hand of your guide, he is responsible to guide you and if not, he is the one responsible, *fī katab al-ʿilmi wa hifshizh bi ghayri ʿamal*, without doing it. That is why it is dangerous. Many, many, many scholars spend their lives writing presentations, but they are not practicing what they learned.

He said, "*aysh yanfʿak*." This is not literary Arabic, it is slang. They put, "I like that as it is important." What is it going to benefit you if you are not doing it and not practicing it? It means, "You donkey!" Spirituality is practice. Even if you practice one *ʿamal* a day, it is better than memorizing thousands of them! And he quoted a *ḥadīth* of the Prophet ﷺ that I like to mention: *yaqūl Allah azza wa jall bi 'l-anbiyā wa 'l-ʿulama*, Allah says on Judgment Day to the prophets and scholars, which means the pious people, "O! If you thought yourself *antum kuntum ru'atu khalqī*, that you are the ones authorized to be shepherds for the nations, what you have done with your flocks? What have you shown them and what have you taught them? You are responsible and you are liable!"

That is why all prophets in Judgment Day, to where do they run? Towards Sayyīdinā Muhammad ﷺ, as what are they going to answer? So if *anbiyā* run to the Prophet ﷺ, where is the *ʿālim* on that Day? Is there any more *ʿālim* then, when even *anbiyā* are shaking there? Where are the *ʿulama* that are sitting on chairs in *dunya* and giving *fatwas*, as if they are the biggest peacocks? They have to run to the Prophet ﷺ, not directly to Allah ﷻ, and if they are not accepting, then they will go directly to Hell!

Today we see too many kings sitting on their chairs like a rooster on his chickens. We also think of ourselves as kings. Ask two people that are similar in their understanding. Will you find that? No, you won't, because each has his own opinion. So the Prophet ﷺ said, "If you are three, put one as *amīr*," but if you do that now they will fight one hour to see who is *amīr*! That is not spirituality, which is *taslīmiyya*, to submit.

Allah ﷻ says to them, *antum kuntum khazān kunuzikum*, "You were the trustees or the guardians of My treasures!" because all the treasures are in the hands of kings. *Hal wasaltum al-fuqara*, "Did you make relations with the poor?"

When Sayyīdinā 'Umar ﷺ became the *khalifah* he was crying and his wife asked him, "Why are you crying? You became *khalifah*."

He said, "Now I have to cry because if anyone is hungry, I am responsible."

He used to carry sacks of food on his back and distribute to the poor people. Today they are kings and queens, yet they are holding the treasures of the world, raising the price of oil and sucking the blood of people! Who raised the price of petroleum in order to build their Gulf nations into prostitution? Go and see there. They built their nations by raising the price of petroleum as a monopoly, while the poor become poorer and the rich become richer.

And that is *ḥadīth* of the Prophet ﷺ quoted by Sayyīdinā Abdul Qadir al-Jilani ق and mentioned in his book, *Kanz al-'Ummāl*. "Did you take care of the poor and did you take care of the *aytam*, orphans?" How much food is sent to orphans and you find it the next day being sold in the market? Allah ﷻ will ask them, "Did you take from your money that is written on you as My right and give to poor people?"

So where do we stand now, are we *Ghulām* or not? We are *Ghulām* now, because we are responsible, but since we are *Ghulām* we are not responsible! It is not me saying this, it is Sayyīdinā Abdul Qadir al-Jilani ق saying it. He will take responsibility for them. One *walī* is enough to take everyone and put in Paradise in *maq'ad sidqin*. Be happy! You think the Prophet ﷺ can be alone in Paradise? He has to have people with him, so be happy, smile! That is *Maqām at-Tashrīf*.

The Difference between an 'Alim and a Wali

We go back to what we were saying. When the Prophet ﷺ went in Ascension he saw Sayyīdinā Musa ﷺ, who always likes to ask questions. He said:

> *Qāla rabbī arinī anzhur ilayk.*
> *He said, "O my Lord! Show Yourself to me that I may look upon You."*
> (Sūrat al-'Arāf, 7:143)

It is so easy for him! Never the Prophet ﷺ has any question, he only listens and obeys. He listened to Sayyīdinā Jibrīl ﷺ. Only one time he had a question: when he left the Seven Heavens and he was going up, he asked

Sayyīdinā Jibrīl ☼, "Are you not coming with me?" to accompany him as a friend.

Sayyīdinā Jibrīl ☼ said, "I cannot."

The Prophet ﷺ moved to the Divine Presence alone. He was in *Maqām at-Tawhīd*. Today "*tawhīd*" is all they speak about! Is Prophet ﷺ going to be exclusively with this group that came recently? What about the Muslims who came before, were they not on *tawhīd*?

Sayyīdinā Musa ☼ said, "*Yā Sayyidī, yā Rasūlullāh!* Can I ask this question, as this comes to my heart all the time. You said '*ulama ummatī ka anbiyā Bani Israel,* '(Genuine) scholars are inheritors of the Prophet ﷺ.'[5] Could it be their knowledge is like our knowledge? Can you give me the answer, *yā Rasūlullāh,* as to how these people are going to inherit from prophets?"

Prophet ﷺ called one through the souls, *fi 'l-arwāh,* as Allah ☼ said, "*Alastu bi rabbikum qālū bala,*" so the Prophet ﷺ can bring any soul he wants from the past and future. He brought one who was to come in the future, after his time, and he said, "That is one."

Sayyīdinā Musa ☼ asked, "What is your name?"

That one said, "Muhammad bin Muhammad bin Muhammad bin Muhammad bin Muhammad bin Muhammad bin Muhammad al-Ghazali," seven times, and if he was able to say it a hundred times he would have, but he felt shy in front of the Prophet ﷺ.

Sayyīdinā Musa ☼ said, "What is this? I thought you were an inheritor of the Prophet ﷺ? Why did you say, 'Muhammad bin Muhammad bin Muhammad bin Muhammad bin Muhammad bin Muhammad bin al-Ghazali'?"

He answered, "If I can say 'Muhammad' until Judgment Day, it will not stop!"[6]

So he said, "*Yā Musa* ☼! Why do you object when I say 'Muhammad bin Muhammad bin Muhammad bin Muhammad bin Muhammad bin Muhammad bin al-Ghazali'? Why didn't you object to your own actions

---

5 Inheritors are not like prophets, but they have knowledge like prophets.

6 As much as you say the name of the Prophet (s), Allah sends angels to say *salāms* on you.

when Allah asked you what is in your hand and you gave all the classifications you are going to use in your lifetime?"

Sayyīdinā Musa ﷺ said, "Because that is place of honor for me to be with the Prophet ﷺ in *Maqām at-Tashrif!"*

So that is the difference between an *'ālim* and a *walī*: how to imitate the Prophet ﷺ and practice his *sunnah*. Practice is important!

In the *ḥadīth* of Sayyīdinā 'Umar ؓ, Prophet ﷺ described *Maqām al-Ihsān*, then Sayyīdinā Jibrīl asked, "Tell me about the Hour, *yā Rasūlullāh*."

Prophet ﷺ said, "The one asked doesn't know more than the one who is asking." That is humbleness; Prophet ﷺ hid his knowledge.

Then Sayyīdinā Jibrīl asked, "Then tell me of its signs."

Prophet ﷺ narrated the signs, including, "The naked, barefooted Bedouins will compete in (building) high buildings."

Now in the deserts of Gulf countries they are competing to erect the tallest building in the world. Are we seeing that or not? There is no more time, O Muslims! Allah shook the Earth three weeks ago and He can shake the Earth whenever He wants to! That was the U.S. stock market crash. That day of judgment is coming, so don't let it cheat us!

Sayyīdinā Abdul Qadir al-Jilani ق also says in this book, "On the Judgment Day a caller will call out, 'Where are the oppressors? Let them come!'"

We are afraid to be oppressors to ourselves! Are we oppressors or not? We don't know for sure, and even he who doesn't know is struggling. If we are not oppressors to ourselves, it means we don't make sins. Do we make sins? Say yes and ask forgiveness, as that is better than saying no. Did we commit hidden *shirk* or not? Anything related to ourselves is hidden *shirk*, such as pride, arrogance, self-praise, etc.

Sayyīdinā Abdul Qadir al-Jilani ق then writes, *ayna awwām adh-dhalama. Ayna man yara min qalaman*, "The oppressors used pens to judge people and send them to prison although they are innocent." *Dhalama* is one who will benefit from anyone, even if they kill people, like in the mafia, which is everywhere now. Today you are afraid not to pay a traffic ticket because they might put you in jail, but what happened to CEOs that sucked billions of dollars from the common people? Are they oppressors or not? Did anyone put them in jail? All those who manipulated the stock market for their gain and harmed so many people will be questioned on Judgment Day, because they made rich people richer and poor people poorer.

Sayyīdinā Abdul Qadir al-Jilani ق continues, "Where is anyone from those who possess a pen? Come here to witness on them, gather them and put them in a casket of fire!"

May Allāh ﷻ forgive us and may Allāh ﷻ bless us.

Wa min Allāhi 't-tawfiq, bi ḥurmati 'l-ḥabīb, bi ḥurmati 'l-Fātiḥah.
And with Allāh is success. For the sake of the Beloved, for his sake we recite the opening chapter of Holy Qur'an.

Islamic Calendar and Holy Days

The Islamic calendar is lunar-based, with twelve months of 29 or 30 days. A lunar year is shorter than a solar year, so Muslim holy days cycle back in the Gregorian (Western) calendar. This is how Ramaḍān is celebrated at different times of the year, as the annual Islamic calendar is ten days shorter than the Gregorian calendar.

Four Islamic months are sacred: Muharram, Rajab, Dhūl-Qʿadah and Dhūl-Hijjah. Holy months include "God's Month" (Rajab), "Prophet's Month" (Shaʿbān) and the "Month of the People" (Ramaḍān), in which pious acts are rewarded more generously.

Months of the Islamic Calendar

1. Muḥarram
2. Safar
3. Rabīʿ ul-Awwal (Rabīʿ I)
4. Rabīʿ uth-Thāni (Rabīʿ II)
5. Jumāda al-Awwal (Jumādi I)
6. Jumāda uth-Thāni (Jumādi II)
7. Rajab
8. Shaʿbān
9. Ramaḍān
10. Shawwāl
11. Dhū'l-Qʿadah
12. Dhū'l-Hijjah

al-Hijra

The 1st of Muharram marks the beginning of the Islamic New Year, chosen because it is the anniversary of Prophet Muḥammad's ﷺ historic *Hijra* (migration) from Mecca to Madinah, where he established the first, preeminent Muslim community in which he introduced unprecedented social reforms, including civil law, human and women's rights, religious tolerance, taxation to serve the community, and military ethics.

ʻAshura

On 10th Muharram, ʻAshūra commemorates many sacred events, such as Noah's ark coming to rest, the birth of Abraham, and the building of the Kaʻbah in Mecca. ʻAshūra is a major holy day, marked with two days of fasting, on the $9^{th}/10^{th}$ or on $10^{th}/11^{th}$ based on a holy tradition (*hadīth*) of Sayyīdinā Muḥammad ﷺ.

Mawlid

Mawlid al-Nabī, 12th Rabiʻ al-Awwal, commemorates Prophet Muḥammad's birth in 570. Mawlid is celebrated globally throughout this month in huge communal gatherings in which a famous poem "Qasīdah al-Burdah" is recited, accompanied by drummers, illustrious poetry recitals, religious singing, eloquent sermons, gift giving, feasts, and feeding the poor. Most Muslim nations observe Mawlid as a national holiday.

Laylat al-Isra wal-Mi'raj

Literally, "the Night Journey and Ascension;" 27th of Rajab is when Sayyīdinā Muḥammad ﷺ physically traveled from Mecca to Jerusalem, ascended in all the levels of Heaven from a rock in the Dome of the Rock, and returned to Mecca—while his bed was still warm. In the Night Journey, Islam's five daily prayers were ordained by God. Sayyīdinā Muḥammad ﷺ also prayed with Abraham, Moses, and Jesus in Jerusalem's al-Aqsa Mosque, signifying that Muslims, Christians, and Jews follow one god. This holy event designated Jerusalem as the third holiest site in Islam, after Mecca and Madinah.

Laylat al-Bara'ah

The "Night of Freedom from Fire" occurs on 15th Shaʻbān. On this night God's Mercy is great; hence, the night is spent reciting Holy Qurʻan and special prayers, as well as visiting the deceased.

Ramadan

Many regard Ramaḍān, the ninth month of the Islamic calendar, the holiest month of the year. Muslims observe a strict fast and participate in pious activities such as charitable giving and peace making. It is a time of intense spiritual renewal for those who observe it. Fasting is meant to instill social awareness of the needy, and to promote gratitude for God's endless favors. The fast is typically broken in a communal setting, and hence Ramaḍān is a highly social month. At night, a special Ramaḍān prayer known as "*Tarawīh*" is offered in congregation, in which one-thirtieth of the Holy Qur'an is recited by the *imām* (prayer leader); thus the entire holy book of six thousand verses is recited in this month.

Eid al-Fitr

"Festival of Fast-Breaking" marks the end of Ramaḍān and is celebrated the first three days of Shawwāl. It is a time for charity and celebration with family and friends for completing a month of blessings and joy. In the Last Days of Ramaḍān, each Muslim family gives "Zakāt al-Fitr"(charity of fast-breaking) which consists of cash and/or food, to help the poor. On the first early morning of Eid, Muslims observe a special congregational prayer, such as Christmas/Easter Mass or the High Holy Days. After Eid prayer is a time to visit family and friends, and give gifts and money (especially to children). Many specialty foods and sweets are prepared solely for Eid days. In most Muslim countries, the entire three days of Eid is a national holiday.

Yawm al-Arafat

"Day of 'Arafat," 9 Dhul-Hijjah, occurs just before the celebration of Eid al-Adha. Pilgrims on Hajj assemble for the "standing" on the plain of 'Arafat, located outside Mecca, where they contemplate the Day of Standing (Resurrection Day). Muslims elsewhere in the world fast this day, and gather at a local mosque for prayers. Thus, those who cannot perform Hajj that year still honor the sacrifice of Abraham.

Eid al-Adha

The "Feast of Sacrifice," celebrated from the 10th-13th Dhul-Hijjah, marks Prophet Abraham's willingness to sacrifice his son Ismāʿīl on God's order. To honor this event, Muslims perform Hajj, the pilgrimage to Mecca that is incumbent on every mature Muslim once in their life if they have the means. Celebrations begin with an animal sacrifice to commemorate Sayyīdinā Abraham's sacrifice. In Islam, he is known as *Khalilullāh,* "God's friend." Many consider him the first Muslim and a premiere role model, for his obedience to God and willingness to sacrifice his only child without even questioning the command.

Glossary

'abd (pl. *'ibād*): lit. slave; servant.
'AbdAllāh: Lit., "servant of God"
Abū Bakr aṣ-Ṣiddīq: the closest Companion of Prophet Muḥammad; the Prophet's father-in-law, who shared the *Hijrah* with him. After the Prophet's death, he was elected the first caliph (successor); known as one of the most saintly Companions.
Abū Yazīd/Bayāzīd Bistāmī: A great ninth century *walī* and a master of the Naqshbandi Golden Chain.
adab: good manners, proper etiquette.
adhān: call to prayer.
Ākhirah: the Hereafter; afterlife.
al-: Arabic definite article, "the".
'alāmīn: world; universes.
Alḥamdūlillāh: praise God.
'Alī ibn Abī Ṭālib: first cousin of Prophet Muḥammad, married to his daughter Fāṭimah; the fourth caliph.
alif: first letter of Arabic alphabet.
'Alīm, al-: the Knower, a divine attribute
Allāh: proper name for God in Arabic.
Allāhu Akbar: God is Greater.
'āmal: good deed (pl. *'amāl*).
amīr (pl., *umarā*): chief, leader, head of a nation or people.
anā: first person singular pronoun
anbīyā: prophets (sing. *nabī*).
'aql: intellect, reason; from the root *'aqila*: lit., "to fetter."
'Arafah, 'Arafat: a plain near Mecca where pilgrims gather for the principal rite of Hajj.
'arif: knower, Gnostic; one who has reached spiritual knowledge of his Lord.
'Ārifūn' bil-Lāh: knowers of God.
Ar-Raḥīm: The Mercy-Giving, Merciful, Munificent, one of Allāh's ninety-nine Holy Names.
Ar-Raḥmān: The Most Merciful, Compassionate, Beneficent; the most repeated of Allāh's Holy Names.
'arsh, al-: the Divine Throne.
aṣl: root, origin, basis.
astāghfirullāh: lit. "I seek Allāh's forgiveness."
Awlīyāullāh: saints of Allāh (sing. *walī*).
āyah (pl. *ayāt*): a verse of the Holy Qur'an.
Āyat al-Kursī: "Verse of the Throne," a well-known supplication from the Qur'an (2:255).
'Azra'īl: the Archangel of Death.
Badī' al-: The Innovator; a Divine Name.
Banī Ādam: Children of Adam; humanity.
Bayt al-Maqdis: the Sacred Mosque in Jerusalem, built at the site where Solomon's Temple was later erected.
Bayt al-Mā'mūr: much-frequented house; this refers to the Ka'bah of the Heavens, which is the prototype of the Ka'bah on Earth, circumambulated by the angels.
baya': pledge; in the context of this book, the pledge of initiation of a disciple (*murīd*) to a shaykh.
Bismillāhi'r-Raḥmāni'r-Raḥīm: "In the name of the All-Merciful, the All-Compassionate"; introductory verse to all chapters of the Qur'an, except the ninth.
Dajjāl: the False Messiah (Anti-Christ) will appear at the end-time of this

world, to deceive Mankind with false divinity.
dalālah: evidence.
dhāt: self / selfhood.
dhawq (pl. *adhwāq*): tasting; technical term referring to the experiential aspect of gnosis.
dhikr: remembrance, mention of God in His Holy Names or phrases of glorification.
dīyā: light.
Diwān al-Awlīyā: the nightly gathering of saints with Prophet Muḥammad in the spiritual realm.
du'ā: supplication.
dunyā: world; worldly life.
'Eid: festival; the two major celebrations of Islam are 'Eid al-Fitr, after Ramaḍān; and 'Eid al-Adha, the Festival of Sacrifice during the time of Hajj, which commemorates the sacrifice of Prophet Abraham.
fard: obligatory worship.
Fātiḥah: Sūratu 'l-Fātiḥah; the opening chapter of the Qur'an.
Ghafūr, al-: The Forgiver; one of the Holy Names of God.
Ghawth: lit. "Helper"; the highest rank of all saints.
ghaybu' l-muṭlaq, al-: the Absolute Unknown; known only to God.
ghusl: full shower/bath obligated by a state of ritual impurity, performed before worship.
Grandshaykh: generally, a *walī* of great stature. In this text, refers to Mawlana 'AbdAllāh ad-Daghestāni (d. 1973), Mawlana Shaykh Nazim's master.
hā': the Arabic letter ه
ḥadīth Nabawī (pl., *aḥadīth*): prophetic tradition whose meaning and linguistic expression are those of Prophet Muḥammad.
Ḥadīth Qudsī: divine saying whose meaning directly reflects the meaning God intended but whose linguistic expression is not divine speech as in the Qur'an.
ḥadr: present
Hajj: the sacred pilgrimage of Islam obligatory on every mature Muslim once in their life.
ḥalāl: permitted, lawful according to Islamic *Sharī'ah*.
Ḥaqīqah, al-: reality of existence; ultimate truth.
ḥaqq: truth
Ḥaqq, al-: the Divine Reality, one of the 99 Divine Names.
ḥarām: forbidden, unlawful.
ḥasanāt: good deeds.
hāshā: God forbid.
ḥarf: (pl. *ḥurūf*) letter; Arabic root "edge."
Ḥawā: Eve.
ḥaywān: animal.
Hijrah: emigration.
ḥikmah: wisdom.
ḥujjah: proof.
hūwa: the pronoun "he,"made up of the Arabic letters *hā'* and *wāw*.
'ibādu 'l-Lāh: servants of God.
'ifrīt: a type of *jinn*, huge and powerful.
iḥsān: doing good, "It is to worship God as though you see Him; for if you are not seeing Him, He sees you."
ikhlāṣ, al-: sincere devotion.
ilāh: (pl. *āliha*): idols or gods.
ilāhīyya: divinity.
ilhām: divine inspiration sent to *awlīyāullāh.*
'ilm: knowledge, science.
'Ilmu 'l-Awrāq: Knowledge of Papers.
'Ilmu 'l-Adhwāq: Knowledge of Taste.
'Ilmu 'l-Hurūf: Science of Letters.

ʿilmu ʿl-kalām: scholastic theology.
ʿilmun ladunnī: divinely inspired knowledge.
imān: faith, belief.
imām: leader of congregational prayer; an advanced scholar followed by a large community.
insān: humanity; pupil of the eye.
insānu ʿl-kāmil, al-: the Perfect Man, *i.e.*, Prophet Muḥammad.
irādatullāh: the Will of God.
irshād: spiritual guidance.
ism: name.
isma-Llāh: name of God.
isrāʿ: night journey; used here in reference to the night journey of Prophet Muḥammad.
Isrāʿfīl: Archangel Rafael, in charge of blowing the Final Trumpet.
jalāl: majesty.
jamāl: beauty.
jamaʿa: group, congregation.
Jannah: Paradise.
jihād: to struggle in God's Path.
Jibrīl: Gabriel, Archangel of revelation.
Jinn: a species of living beings created from fire, invisible to most humans. *Jinns* can be Muslim or non-Muslim.
Jumuʿah: Friday congregational prayer, held in a large mosque.
Kaʿbah: the first House of God, located in Mecca, Saudi Arabia to which pilgrimage is made and to which Muslims face in prayer.
kāfir: unbeliever.
Kalāmullāh al-Qadīm: lit., Allāh's Ancient Words, *viz.* the Holy Qur'an.
kalīmat at-tawḥīd: lā ilāha illa-Llāh: "There is no god but Al-Lāh (the God)."
karāmat: miracles.
khalīfah: deputy.
Khāliq, al-: the Creator, one of 99 Divine Names.
khalq: Creation.
khāniqah: designated smaller place for worship other than a mosque; *zāwiyah.*
khuluq: conduct, manners.
Kirāmun Kātabīn: honored Scribe angels.
lā: no; not; not existent; the particle of negation.
lā ilāha illa-Llāh Muḥammadun Rasūlullāh: There is no deity except Allāh, Muḥammad is the Messenger of Allāh.
lām: Arabic letter ل.
al-Lawḥ al-Maḥfūẓ: the Preserved Tablets.
Laylat al-Isrāʿ wa'l-Miʿrāj: the Night Journey and Ascension of Prophet Muḥammad to Jerusalem and to the Seven Heavens.
Madīnātu ʿl-Munawwara: the Illuminated city; city of Prophet Muḥammad; Madinah.
mahr: dowry, given by the groom to the bride.
malakūt: Divine Kingdom.
Malik, al-: the Sovereign, a Divine Name.
Mālik: Archangel of Hell.
maqām: spiritual station; tomb of a prophet, messenger or saint.
maʿrifah: gnosis.
Māshā'Allāh: as Allāh Wills.
Mawlānā: lit. "Our master" or "our patron,"referring to an esteemed person.
maẓhar: place of disclosure.
miḥrāb: prayer niche.
Mikāʿīl: Michael, Archangel of rain.
mīzān: the scale that weighs our deeds on Judgment Day.
mīm: Arabic letter م.

minbar: pulpit.
Miracles: of saints, known as *karamāt*; of prophets, known as *mu'jizāt* (lit., "That which renders powerless or helpless").
mi'rāj: the ascension of Prophet Muḥammad from Jerusalem to the Seven Heavens.
Muḥammadun rasūlu 'l-Lāh: Muḥammad is the Messenger of God.
mulk, al-: the World of dominion.
Mu'min, al-: Guardian of Faith, one of the 99 Names of God.
mu'min: a believer.
munājāt: invocation to God in a very intimate form.
Munkir: one of the angels of the grave.
murīd: disciple, student, follower.
murshid: spiritual guide; *pir*.
mushāhadah: direct witnessing.
mushrik (pl. *mushrikūn*): idolater; polytheist.
muwwāḥid (pl. *muwāḥḥidūn*): those who affirm God's Oneness.
nabī: a prophet of God.
nafs: lower self, ego.
Nakīr: the other angel of the grave (with Munkir).
nūr: light.
Nūḥ: the prophet Noah.
Nūr, an-: "The Source of Light"; a Divine Name.
Qādir, al-: "The Powerful"; a Divine Name.
qalam, al-: the Pen.
qiblah: direction, specifically, the direction faced by Muslims during prayer and other worship, towards the Sacred House in Mecca.
Quddūs, al-: "The Holy One"; a Divine Name.
qurb: nearness
quṭb (pl. *aqṭāb*): axis or pole. Among the poles are:
Quṭbu 'l-Bilād: Pole of the Lands.
Quṭbu 'l-Irshād: Pole of Guidance.
Quṭbu 'l-Aqṭāb: Pole of Poles.
Quṭbu 'l-A'dham: Highest Pole.
Quṭbu 'l-Mutaṣarrif: Pole of Affairs.
al-quṭbīyyatu 'l-kubrā: the highest station of poleship.
Rabb, ar-: the Lord.
Raḥīm, ar-: "The Most Compassionate"; a Divine Name.
Raḥmān, ar-: "The All-Merciful"; a Divine Name.
raḥmā: mercy.
raka'at: one full set of prescribed motions in prayer. Each prayer consists of a one or more *raka'ats.*
Ramaḍān: the ninth month of the Islamic calendar; month of fasting.
Rasūl: a messenger of God.
Rasūlullāh: the Messenger of God, Muḥammad ﷺ.
Ra'ūf, ar-: "The Most Kind"; a Divine Name.
Razzāq, ar-: "The Provider"; a Divine Name.
rawḥānīyyah: spirituality; spiritual essence of something.
Riḍwān: Archangel of Paradise.
rizq: provision; sustenance.
rūḥ: spirit. *Ar-Rūḥ* is the name of a great angel.
rukū': bowing posture of the prayer.
ṣadaqah: voluntary charity.
Ṣaḥābah (sing., *ṣaḥābī*): Companions of the Prophet; the first Muslims.
ṣaḥīḥ: authentic; term certifying validity of a *ḥadīth* of the Prophet.
ṣāim: fasting person (pl. *ṣāimūn*)
sajda (pl. *sujūd*): prostration.
ṣalāt: ritual prayer, one of the five obligatory pillars of Islam. Also, to invoke blessing on the Prophet.

Ṣalāt an-Najāt: prayer of salvation, offered in the late hours of night.
ṣalawāt (sing. *ṣalāt*): invoking blessings and peace upon the Prophet.
salām: peace.
Salām, as-: "The Peaceful"; a Divine Name. *As-salāmu 'alaykum:* "Peace be upon you," the Islamic greeting.
Ṣamad, aṣ-: Self-Sufficient, upon whom creatures depend.
ṣawm, ṣiyām: fasting.
sayyi'āt: bad deeds; sins.
sayyid: leader; also, a descendant of Prophet Muḥammad.
Sayyīdinā: our master (fem. *sayyidunā; sayyidatunā*: our mistress).
shahādah: lit. testimony; the testimony of Islamic faith: *lā ilāha illa 'l-Lāh wa Muḥammadun rasūlu 'l-Lāh*, "There is no god but Allāh, the One God, and Muḥammad is the Messenger of God."
Shah Naqshband: Muḥammad Bahauddin Shah Naqshband, a great eighth century *walī*, and the founder of the Naqshbandi Ṭarīqah.
shaykh: lit. "old Man," a religious guide, teacher; master of spiritual discipline.
shifā': cure.
shirk: polytheism, idolatry, ascribing partners to God
ṣiffāt: attributes; term referring to Divine Attributes.
Silsilat adh-dhahabīyya: "Golden Chain"of spiritual authority in Islam
sohbet (Arabic, *suḥbah*): association: the assembly or discourse of a shaykh.
subḥānAllāh: glory be to God.
sulṭān/sulṭānah: ruler, monarch.
Sulṭān al-Awlīyā: lit., "King of the *awlīyā*; the highest-ranking saint.
Sūnnah: Practices of Prophet Muḥammad in actions and words; what he did, said, recommended, or approved of in his Companions.
sūrah: a chapter of the Qur'an; picture, image.
Sūratu 'l-Ikhlāṣ: Chapter 114 of Holy Qur'an; the Chapter of Sincerity.
ṭabīb: doctor.
tābi'īn: the Successors, one generation after the Prophet's Companions.
tafsīr: to explain, expound, explicate, or interpret; technical term for commentary or exegesis of the Holy Qur'an.
tajallī (pl. *tajallīyāt*): theophanies, God's self-disclosures, Divine Self-manifestation.
takbīr: lit. *"Allāhu Akbar,"*God is Great.
tarawīḥ: the special nightly prayers of Ramaḍān.
ṭarīqat/ṭarīqah: lit., way, road or path. An Islamic order or path of discipline and devotion under a guide or shaykh; Sufism.
taṣbīḥ: recitation glorifying or praising God.
tawāḍa': humbleness.
ṭawāf: the rite of circumambulating the Ka'bah while glorifying God during Hajj and 'Umra.
tawḥīd: unity; universal or primordial Islam, submission to God, as the sole Master of destiny and ultimate Reality.
Tawrāt: Torah
tayammum: Alternate ritual ablution performed in the absence of water.
'ubūdīyyah: state of worshipfulness; servanthood.
'ulamā (sing. *'ālim*): scholars.
'ulūmu 'l-awwalīna wa 'l-ākhirīn: Knowledge of the "Firsts"and the

"Lasts" refers to the knowledge God poured into the heart of Prophet Muḥammad during his Holy Ascension to the Divine Presence.
ʿulūm al-Islāmī: Islamic religious sciences.
Ummāh: faith community, nation.
ʿUmar ibn al-Khaṭṭāb: an eminent Companion of Prophet Muḥammad and second caliph of Islam.
ʿumra: the minor pilgrimage to Mecca, performed at any time of the year.
ʿUthmān ibn ʿAffān: eminent Companion of the Prophet; his son-in-law and third caliph of Islam, renowned for compiling the Qur'an.
walad: a child.
waladī: my child.
walāyah: proximity or closeness; sainthood.
walī (pl. *awlīyā*): saint, or "he who assists"; guardian; protector.
wasīlah: a means; holy station of Prophet Muḥammad as God's intermediary to grant supplications.
wāw: Arabic letter و
wujūd, al-: existence; "to find," "the act of finding," and "being found."
Yʿaqūb: Jacob; the prophet.
yamīn: the right hand; previously meant "oath."
Yawm al-ʿahdi waʾl-mīthāq: Day of Oath and Covenant, a heavenly event before this Life, when all souls of humanity were present to God, and He took from each the promise to accept His Sovereignty as Lord.
yawm al-qiyāmah: Day of Judgment.
Yūsuf: Joseph; the prophet.
zāwiyah: designated smaller place for worship other than a mosque; also *khāniqah.*
zīyāra: visitation to the grave of a prophet, a prophet's companion or a saint.

Other Publications Available at www.isn1.net

Mawlana Shaykh Nazim Adil al-Haqqani

- Heavenly Showers (2012)
- The Sufilive Series (2010-2011)
- Breaths from Beyond the Curtain (2010)
- In the Eye of the Needle
- The Healing Power of Sufi Meditation
- The Path to Spiritual Excellence
- In the Mystic Footsteps of Saints (2 volumes)
- Liberating the Soul (6 volumes)

Shaykh Hisham Kabbani

- The Prohibition of Domestic Violence in Islam (2011)
- The Sufilive Series (2010-2011)
- Cyprus Summer Series (2 volumes)
- The Nine-fold Ascent
- Who Are the Guides?
- Illuminations
- Banquet for the Soul
- Symphony of Remembrance
- The Healing Power of Sufi Meditation
- In the Shadow of Saints
- Keys to the Divine Kingdom
- The Sufi Science of Self-Realization
- Universe Rising: the Approach of Armageddon?
- Pearls and Coral (2 volumes)
- Classical Islam and the Naqshbandi Sufi Tradition
- The Naqshbandi Sufi Way
- Encyclopedia of Islamic Doctrine (7 volumes)
- Angels Unveiled
- Encyclopedia of Muḥammad's Women Companions and the Traditions They Related

Hajjah Amina Adil

- Muḥammad: the Messenger of Islam
- The Light of Muḥammad
- Lore of Light / Links of Light
- My Little Lore of Light (3 volumes)

Hajjah Naziha Adil Kabbani

- Secrets of Heavenly Food (2009)
- Heavenly Foods (2011)

Lightning Source UK Ltd.
Milton Keynes UK
UKOW042006220313

207975UK00005B/16/P

9 781930 409989